MACHINIST FIRST YEAR MCQ

OBJECTIVE QUESTION ANSWERS

MANOJ DOLE

Made with ♥ on the Notion Press Platform
www.notionpress.com

Digitization is the need of the time. In the future, training in industrial training institutes will need to be conducted using online internet to make training more convenient and easy. E-books containing a set of MCQ questions will be made available to the trainees as they need to be more accustomed to the multiple choice questions MCQ to prepare for the online exams taking place in their industrial training institutes.

With all these factors in mind, Mr. Manoj Madhukar Dole Instructor, Industrial Training Institute, Satara, has written books according to the new annual system and NSQF-5 syllabus. And they've created theoretical mobile apps and blogs to make training easier, and made all these educational materials available for download on the world famous websites Google Play Store, Amazon and Apple Book Store.

The books were published by Hon'ble Joint Director Shri Rajendra Ghume Saheb Regional Office of Vocational Education and Training, Pune on 9/1/2019, at this time Shri Prakash Saigavkar Saheb Principal Government Industrial Training Institute Aundh Pune, Shri Tukaram Misal Saheb Principal Govt. Q. Sanstha Satara, Shri Sachin Dhumal Saheb District Vocational Education and Training Officer Satara, Shri Yatin Pargaonkar Saheb Principal Govt. Q. Sanstha Kolhapur, Shri Vikas Teke Saheb Inspector Vocational Education and Training Regional Office Pune, Palekar Foods Products Pvt. Ltd. Entrepreneurial Chairman of Satara Mr. Nilkanthrao Palekar Saheb, Chairman of Hira Foods Mr. Ibrahim Baba Tamboli Saheb, Mrs. Shalmali Pawar Headmaster Government Technical School Center Satara and other dignitaries were present on the occasion.

Contents

Prologue

Machinist First Year MCQ is a simple e-Book for ITI & Engineering Course Lift and Escalator Mechanic, First Year, Sem- 1 & 2, Revised NSQ F-5 Syllabus in 2022, It contains objective questions with underlined & bold correct answers MCQ covering all topics including all about the latest & Important about safety aspect related to the trade, basic fitting operations viz., making, filing, sawing, chiseling, drilling, tapping, grinding, different fits viz., sliding, T-fit and square fit, Lathe operation, turning operation including thread cutting, slotting machine and making different components, conventional milling machine with extensive coverage of different operations viz., plain, face, angular, form, gauge, straddle milling, square thread cutting, grinding operation (both surface and cylindrical) and lots more.

We add new question answers with each new version. Please email us in case of any errors/omissions. This is arguably the largest and best e-Book for All engineering multiple choice questions and answers.

As a student you can use it for your exam prep. This e-Book is also useful for professors to refresh material.

Foreword

Vocational education and training is imparted through the Department of Vocational Education and Training through the Department of Business Education and Business Practical to supply multi-skilled artisans in line with the rapidly growing demand in the industrial sector in the 21st century. All the occupations within the institutions are important, as the trainees from these occupations develop multi-skills as per the demands of the industry.

with the noble intention of making available MCQ e-books suitable for all businesses, considering that all the examinations in all the industries in the industrial sector are conducted online and include MCQ method questions. Mr. Manoj Madhukar Dole has written a very good e-book on MCQ method as per the new annual syllabus. This e-book will definitely be a guide for all the trainees, trainee candidates, training instructors and others concerned.

The author of the book is Mr. Manoj Madhukar Dole, Instructor Gov. ITI Satara has 17 years of training experience. Written as a new annual pattern, this e-book incorporates modern digital QR Code technology to understand the layout, simple language, and simple syntax, diagrams and videos for each subject. So I am sure that this e-book will definitely be useful for in-depth study and exam practice. The work they have done is certainly commendable.

Mr. Tukaram Misal
Principal Government Industrial Training Institute Satara.

Preface

DGET New Delhi and CSTARI Kolkata have been implementing an annual pattern for all businesses in ITI since the August 2018 session. The examination system will also be changed and it will be online from this year and since all the questions are of Objective Type (MCQ), the trainees are in dire need of in-depth study. It is with this in mind that we are delighted to present the books based on the old NIMI pattern and a complete overview of the new annual pattern, and we hope that these books will be a guide for all business directors and trainees. Is.

For writing these books, Johar Awate Saheb, Principal of ITI Akluj. Former Principal of ITI Satara Saigavkar Saheb, Assistant Director Shri Chandrakant Dhekne Saheb Regional Office of Vocational Education and Training, Pune, District Vocational Education and Training Officer Sachin Dhumal Saheb and Headmaster Government Technical School Kendra Shalmali Pawar Madam and son Adhiraj Dole, mother Kusum Dole, I am very grateful to my father Madhukar Dole and wife Ashwini Dole for their special guidance and cooperation from time to time.

Also, in a very short period of time, the book was reviewed by Shri Rajendra Ghume Saheb, Joint Director, Vocational Education and Training Regional Office, Pune, for his invaluable time in publishing the book. I am sincerely grateful for their feedback.

I am grateful to the Instructor of ITI Satara for there continuous support from the very beginning of writing the book.

From this book, I consider myself blessed to have shared my thoughts on e-learning with you. I will not claim that this book is perfect, because considering the perfection, this book is an attempt and is in its infancy. They will be valuable for improvement if they are tested and suggested.

Manoj Dole
Dated 9/1/2019

Acknowledgements

The industrial training and theoretical examination system of our industrial training institutes and these changes have been accepted by the craft instructors and the trainees. Theoretical examinations conducted in your industrial training institutes are also conducted online. Since these examinations are of multiple choice MCQ method, the trainees will need to get more practice of such questions.

With all these considerations in mind, Mr. Manoj Madhukar, Director, Dole Crafts, Katari Industrial Training Institute, Satara, has done a thorough study and with his diligent work and added his keen intellect, according to the new annual system and NSQF-5 syllabus, e-book of Katari and other machine trades. -Book) and they have created mobile apps and blogs on theoretical topics to make training easier and have made all these educational materials available for download on the world famous websites Google Play Store, Amazon and Apple Book Store. Training has been made easier by creating a print version and using advanced techniques like QR Code.

All these educational materials will definitely be a guide for all the trainees for in-depth study and for the craft instructors and other concerned who are imparting vocational training.

CHAPTER ONE

Machinist First Year MCQ Drawings

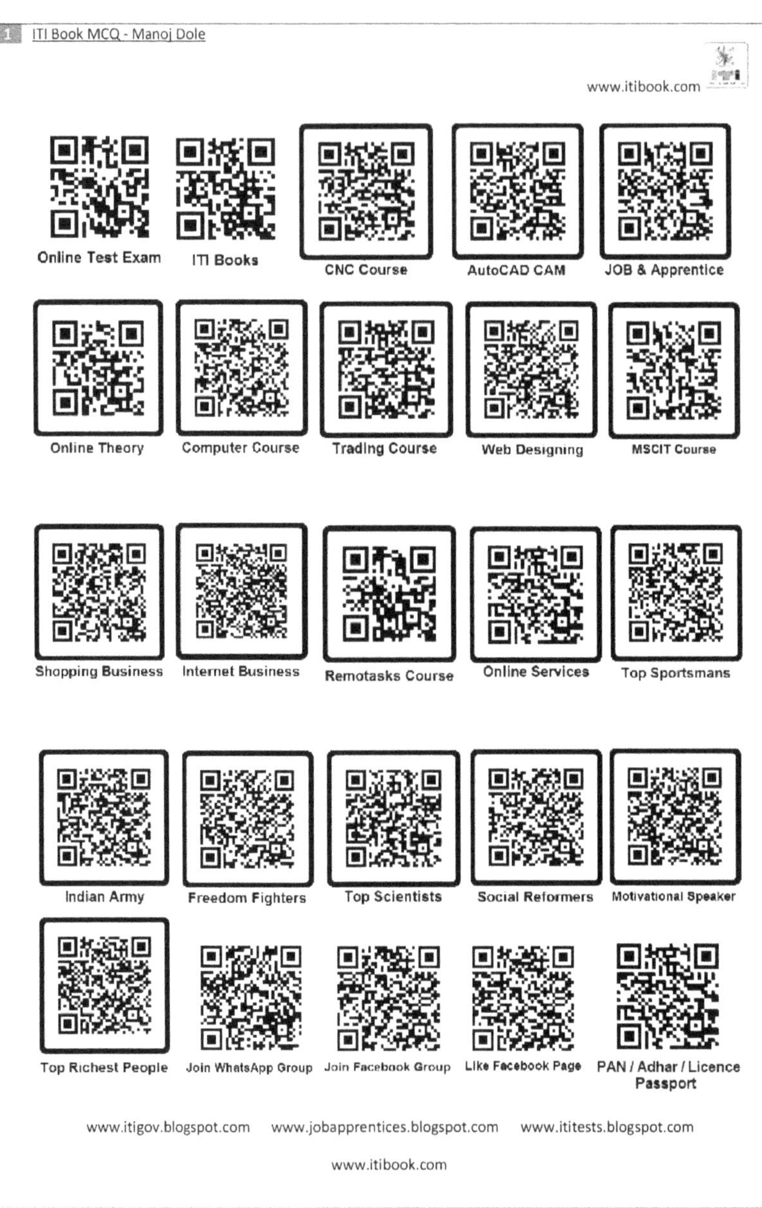
1 ITI Book MCQ - Manoj Dole
www.itibook.com
Online Test Exam
ITI Books
CNC Course
AutoCAD CAM
JOB & Apprentice
Online Theory
Computer Course
Trading Course
Web Designing
MSCIT Course
Shopping Business
Internet Business
Remotasks Course
Online Services
Top Sportsmans
Indian Army
Freedom Fighters
Top Scientists
Social Reformers
Motivational Speaker
Top Richest People
Join WhatsApp Group
Join Facebook Group
Like Facebook Page
PAN / Adhar / Licence Passport
www.itigov.blogspot.com
www.jobapprentices.blogspot.com
www.ititests.blogspot.com
www.itibook.com

www.itibook.com

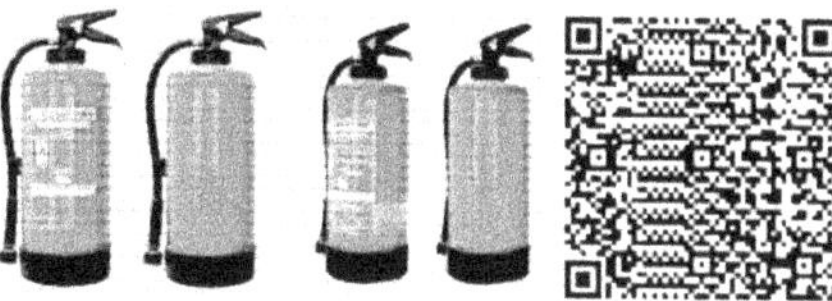

Fire extinguisher

Calliper

Hacksaw frame

Universal surface guage

Hammer

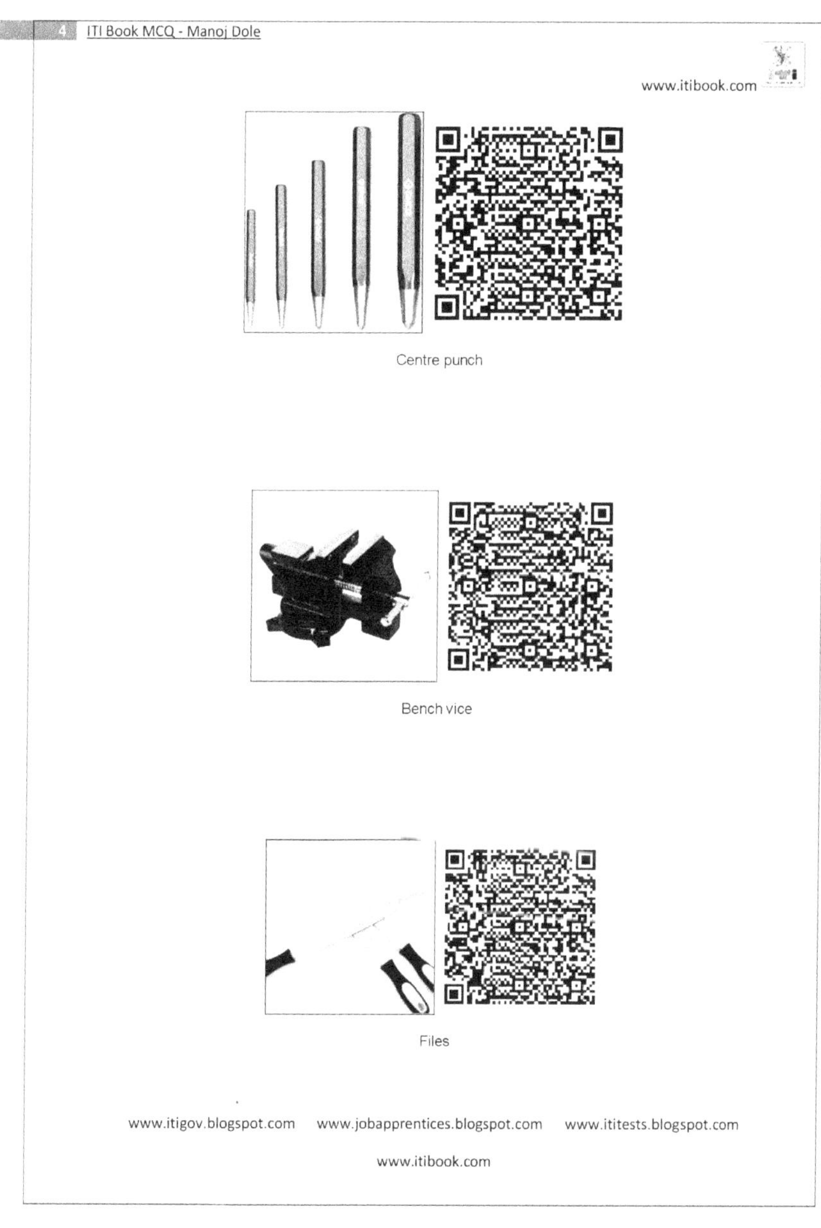

Centre punch

Bench vice

Files

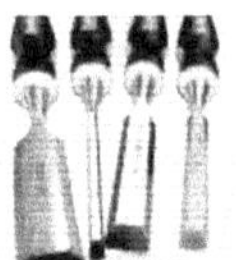 

Scraper

Surface Plate

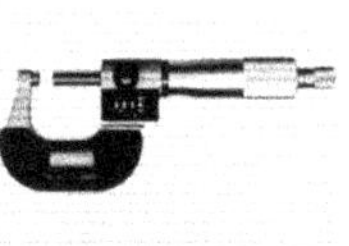 

Outside Micrometer

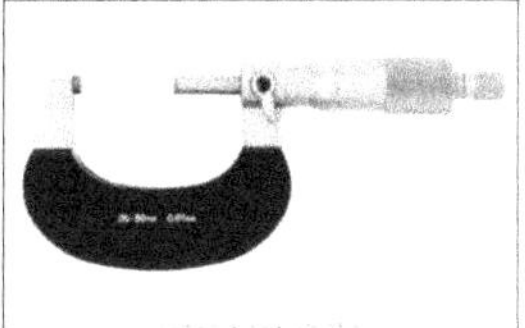

Micrometer

Depth micrometer

Vernier Calliper

Vernier bevel protractor

Drilling

Reamer

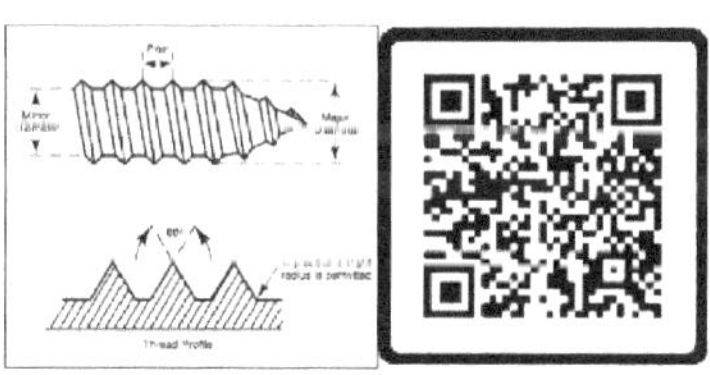

Thread

Tap Die

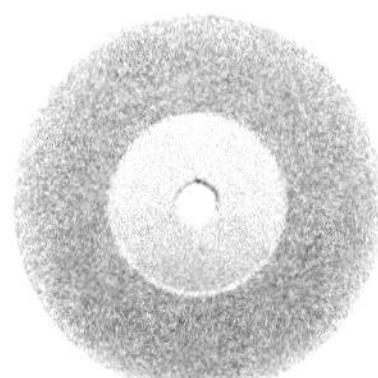

Grinding Wheel

Slip gauge

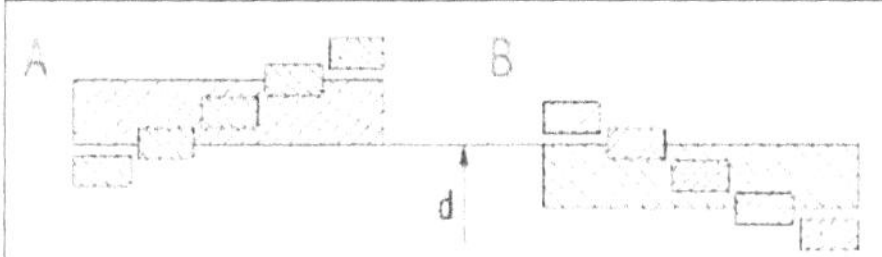

Limit fit tolerance

Lathe Machine

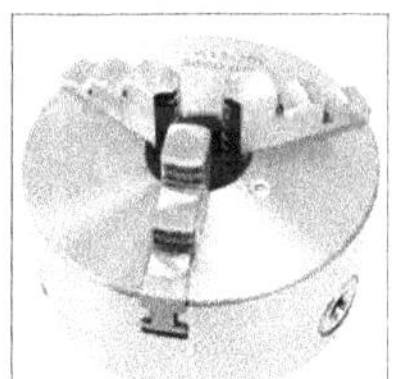

Lathe chuck

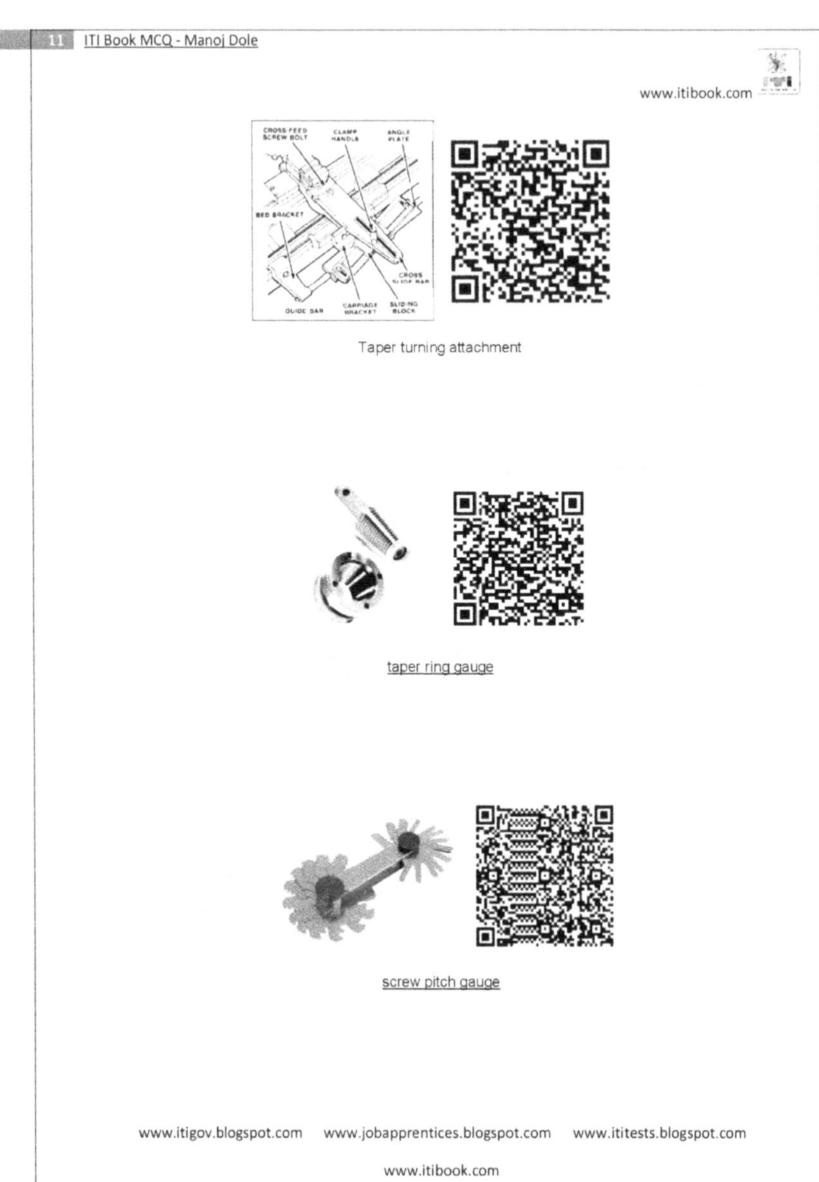

www.itibook.com

Taper turning attachment

taper ring gauge

screw pitch gauge

www.itigov.blogspot.com www.jobapprentices.blogspot.com www.ititests.blogspot.com

www.itibook.com

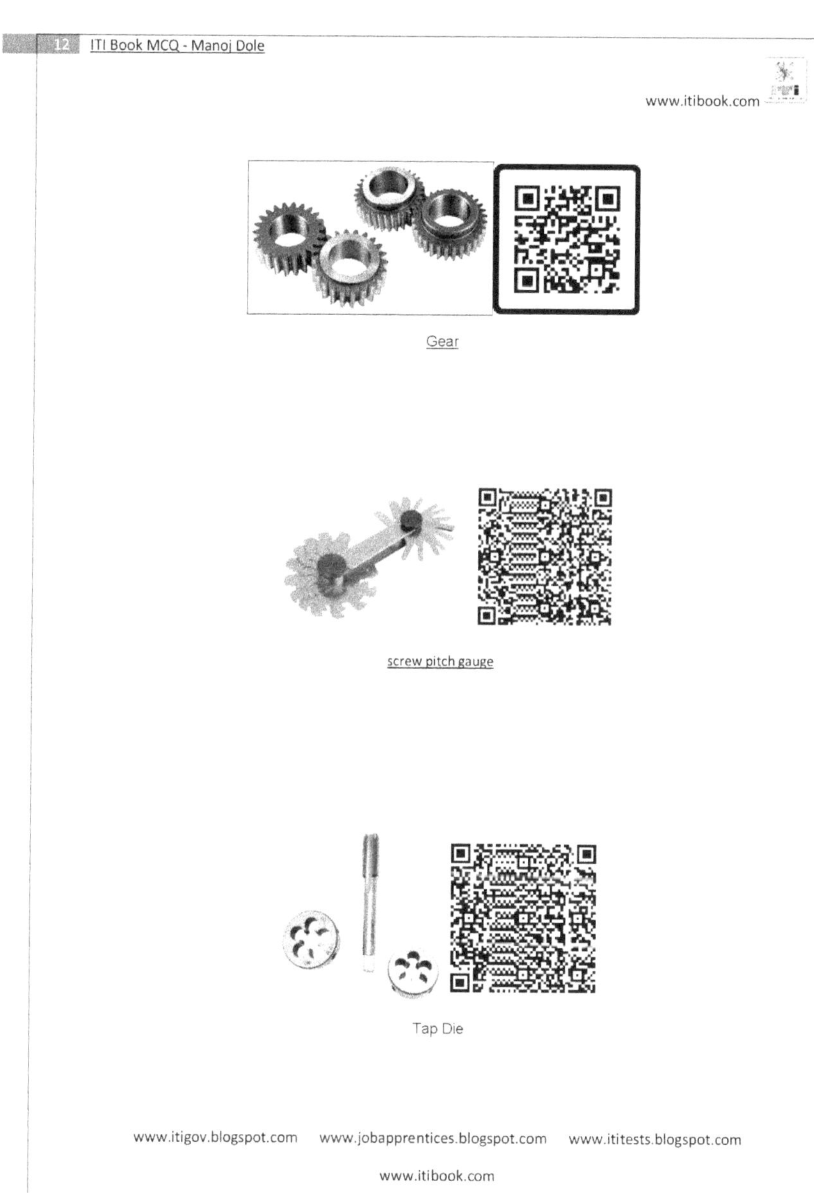

Gear

screw pitch gauge

Tap Die

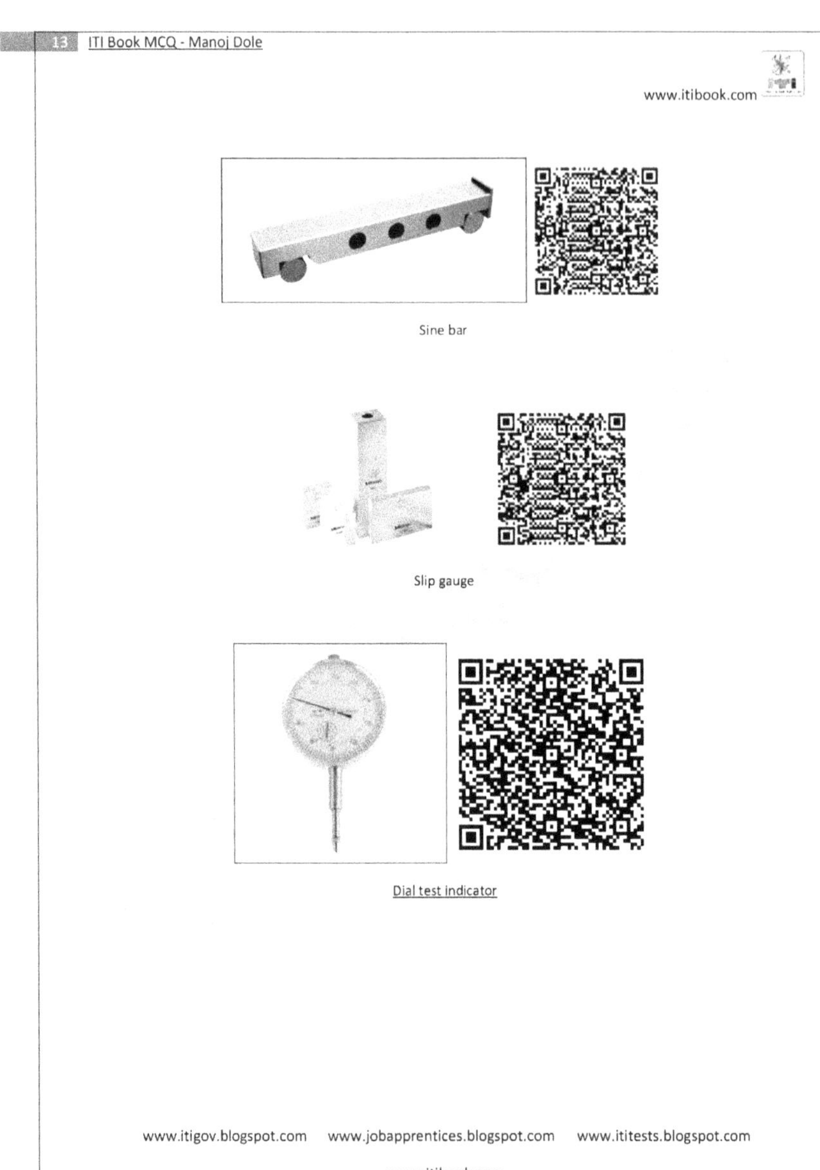
13 ITI Book MCQ - Manoj Dole
www.itibook.com
Sine bar
Slip gauge
Dial test indicator
www.itigov.blogspot.com www.jobapprentices.blogspot.com www.ititests.blogspot.com
www.itibook.com

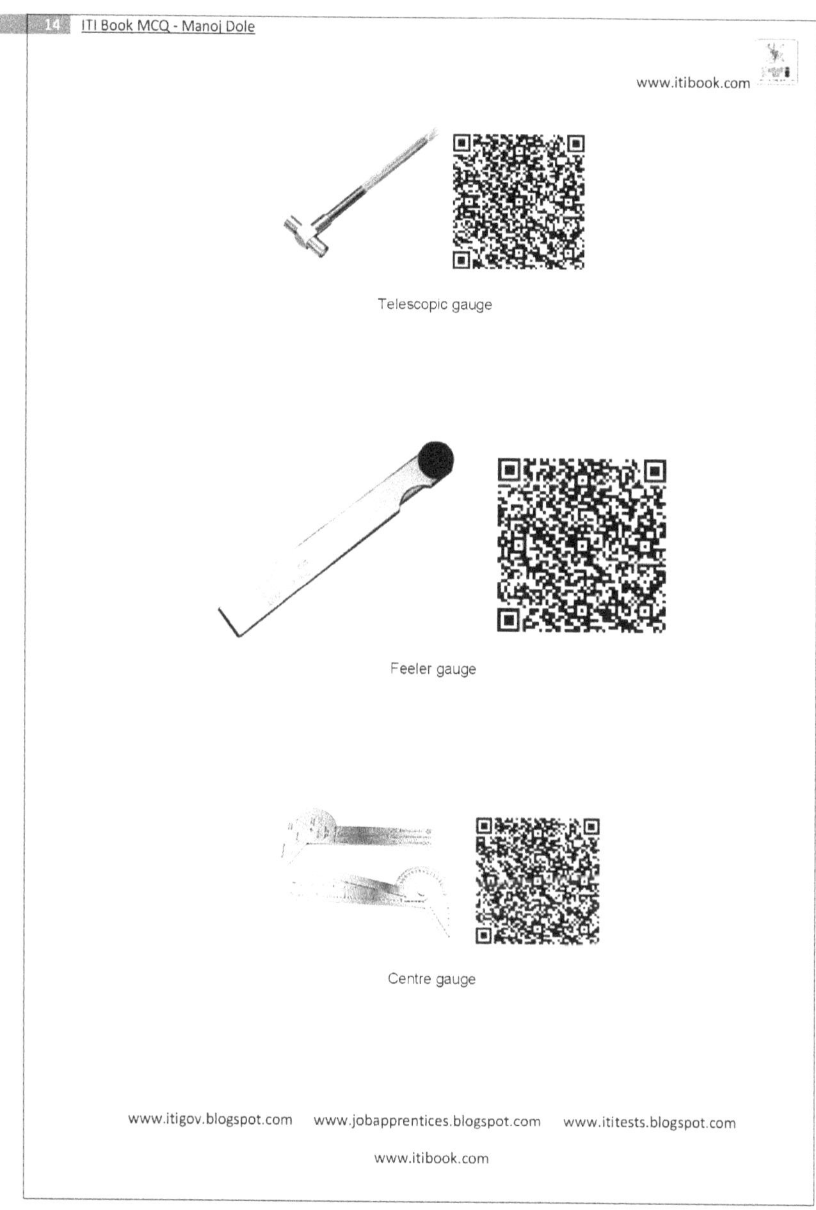

Telescopic gauge

Feeler gauge

Centre gauge

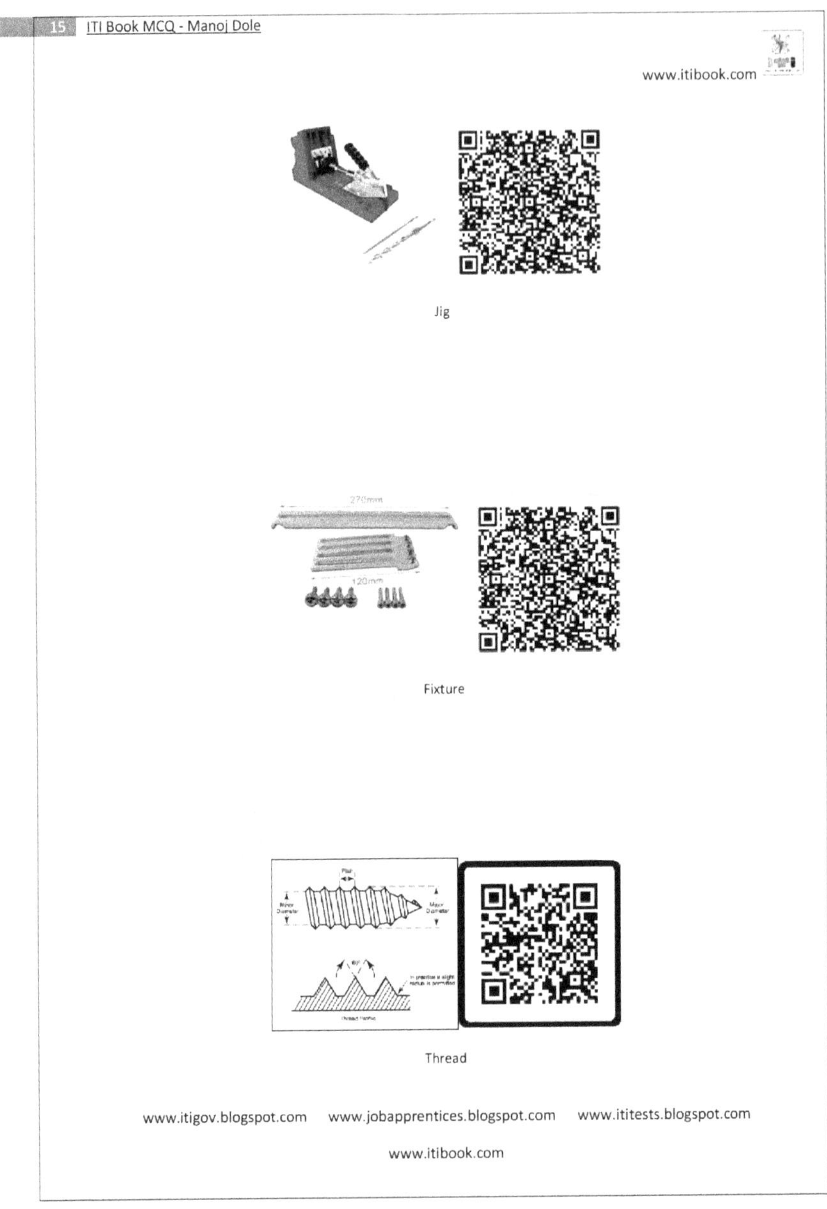

15 ITI Book MCQ - Manoj Dole

www.itibook.com

Jig

Fixture

Thread

www.itigov.blogspot.com www.jobapprentices.blogspot.com www.ititests.blogspot.com

www.itibook.com

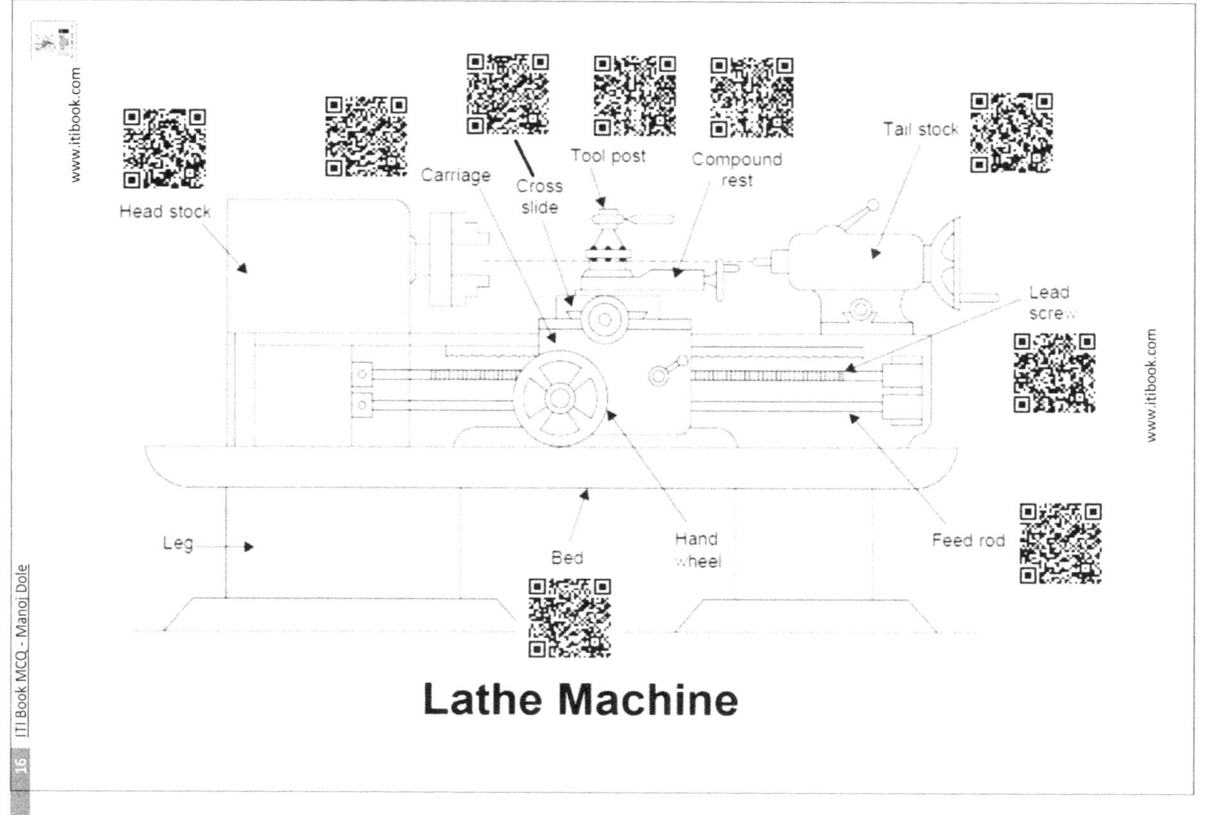
16 ITI Book MCQ - Manoj Dole
www.itibook.com
Head stock
Carriage
Cross slide
Tool post
Compound rest
Tail stock
Lead screw
Leg
Bed
Hand wheel
Feed rod
Lathe Machine
www.itibook.com

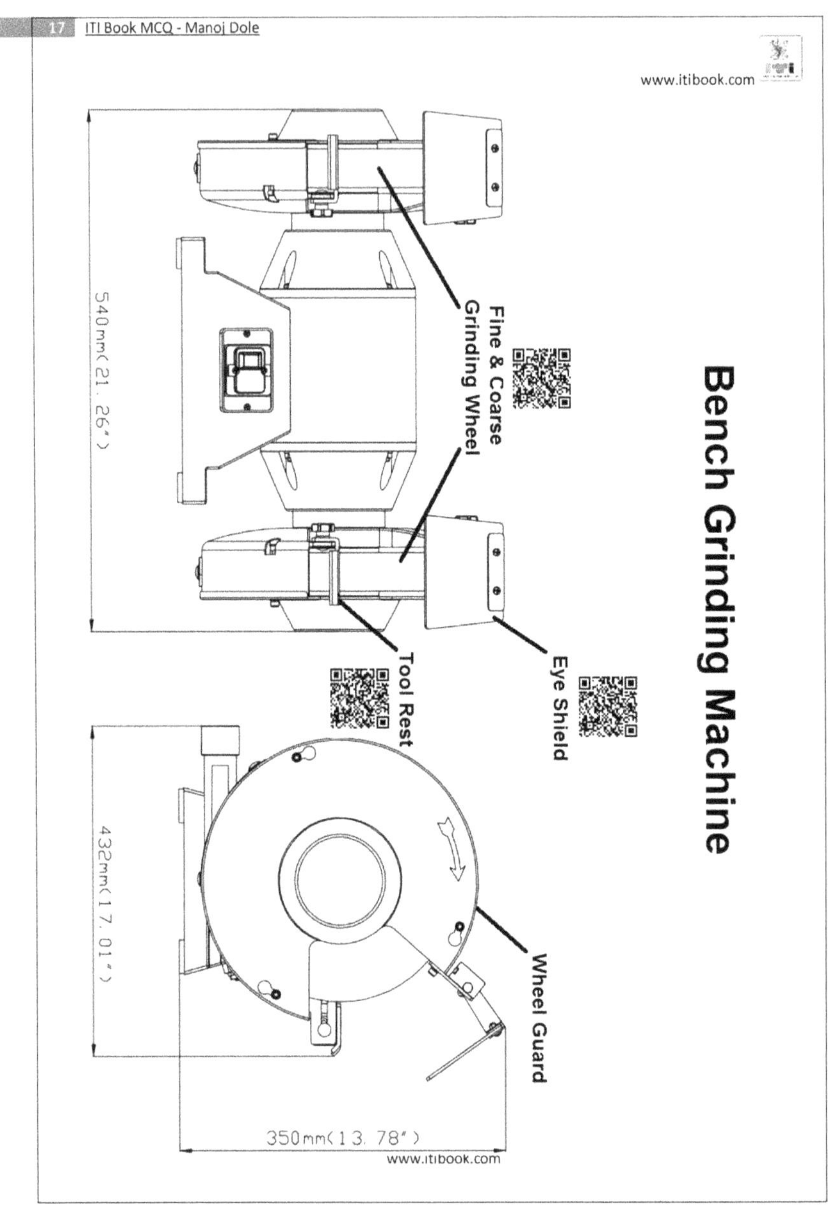
17 ITI Book MCQ - Manoj Dole
www.itibook.com
Bench Grinding Machine
Fine & Coarse Grinding Wheel
Eye Shield
Tool Rest
Wheel Guard
540mm(21.26")
432mm(17.01")
350mm(13.78")
www.itibook.com

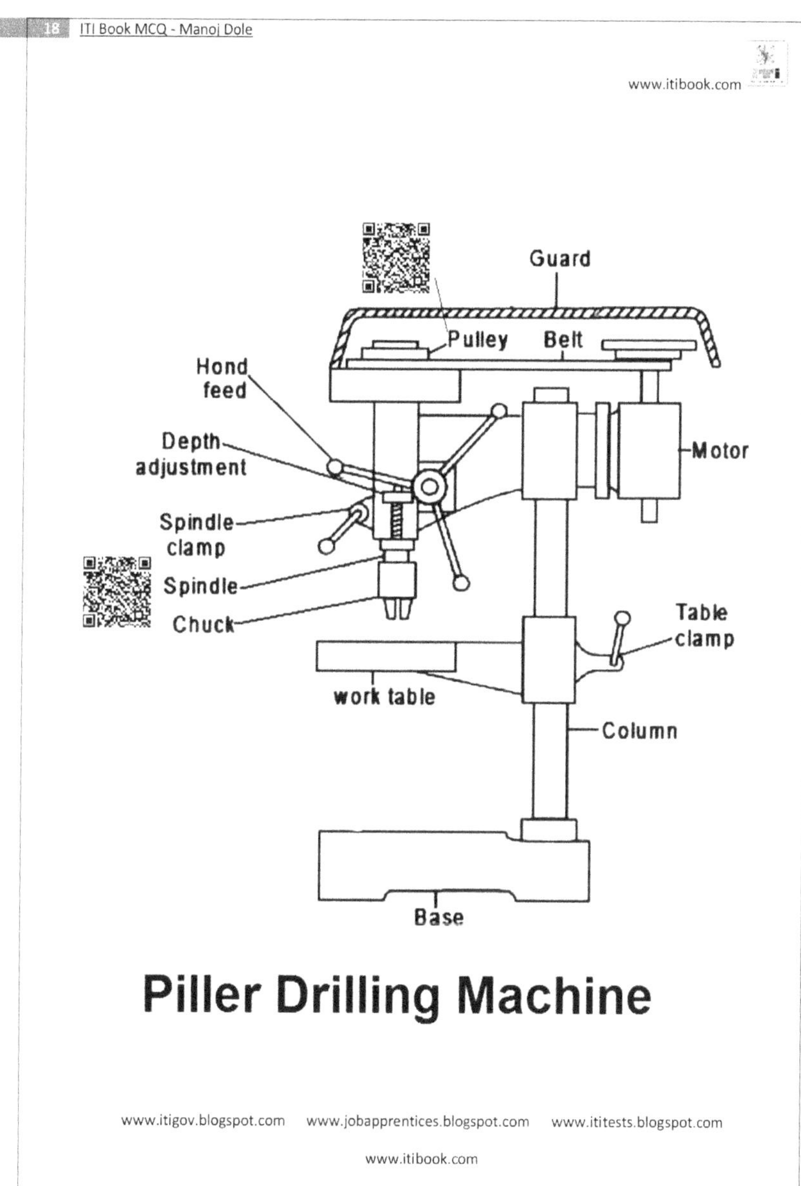
18 ITI Book MCQ - Manoj Dole
www.itibook.com
Guard
Pulley
Belt
Hond feed
Depth adjustment
Motor
Spindle clamp
Spindle
Chuck
Table clamp
work table
Column
Base
Piller Drilling Machine
www.itigov.blogspot.com
www.jobapprentices.blogspot.com
www.ititests.blogspot.com
www.itibook.com

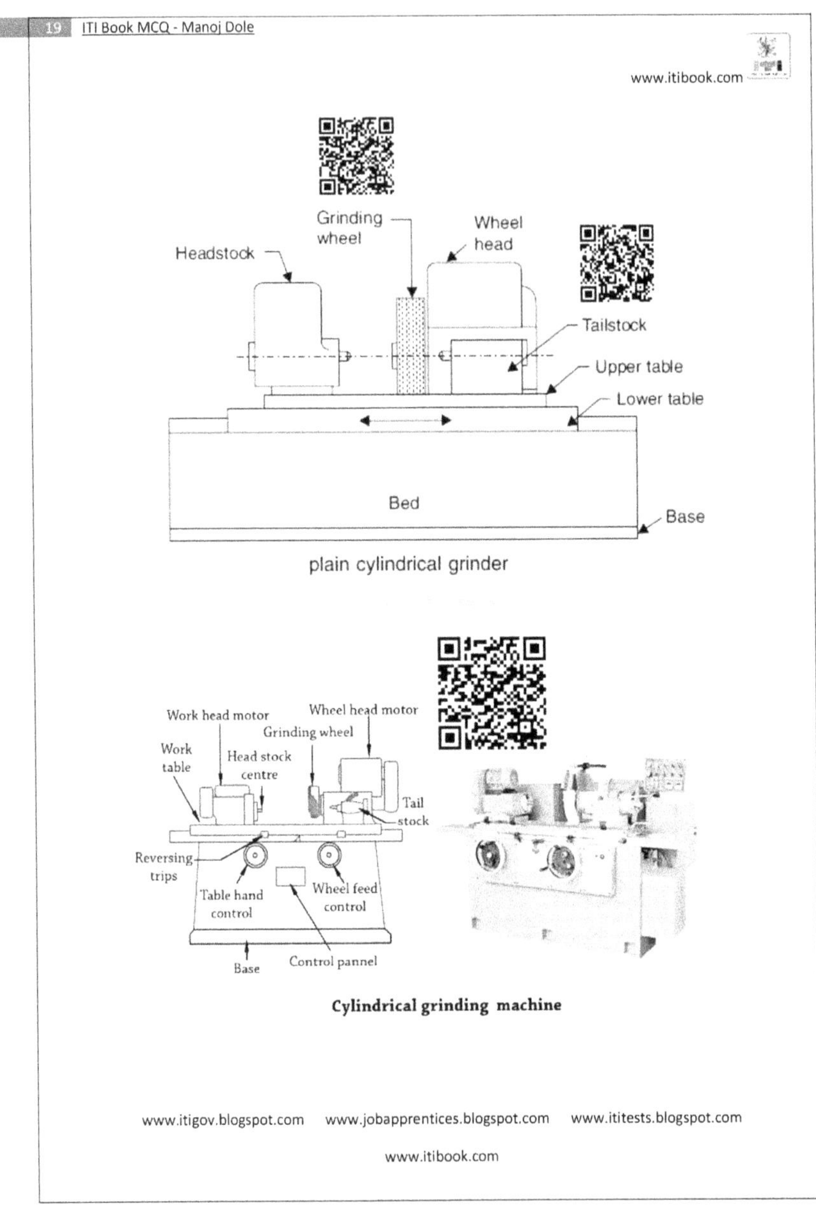

plain cylindrical grinder

Cylindrical grinding machine

To study Different operations and parts of Surface Grinding Machine

SURFACE GRINDER

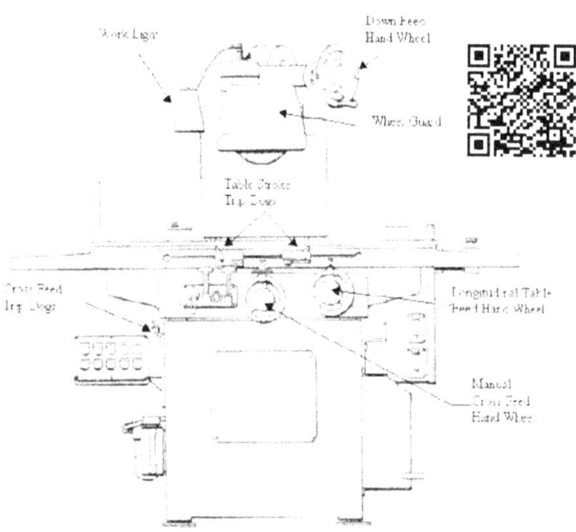

Surface grinding is used to produce a smooth finish on flat surfaces. It is a widely used abrasive machining process in which a spinning wheel covered in rough particles (grinding wheel) cuts

PLAIN OR HORIZONTAL MILLING MACHINE

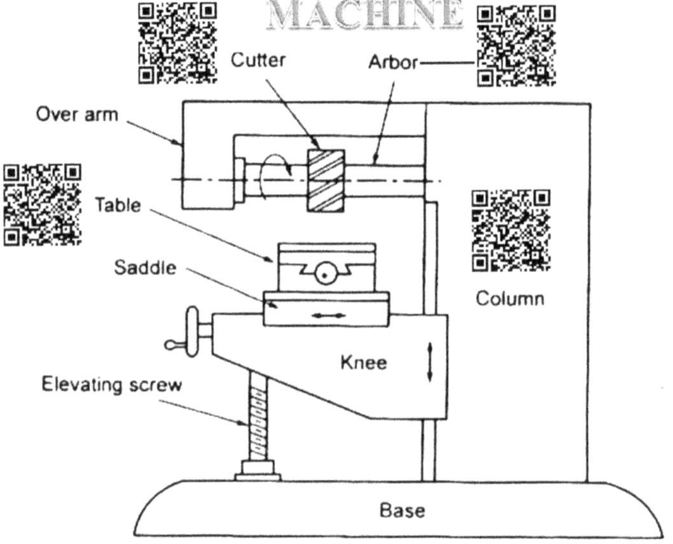

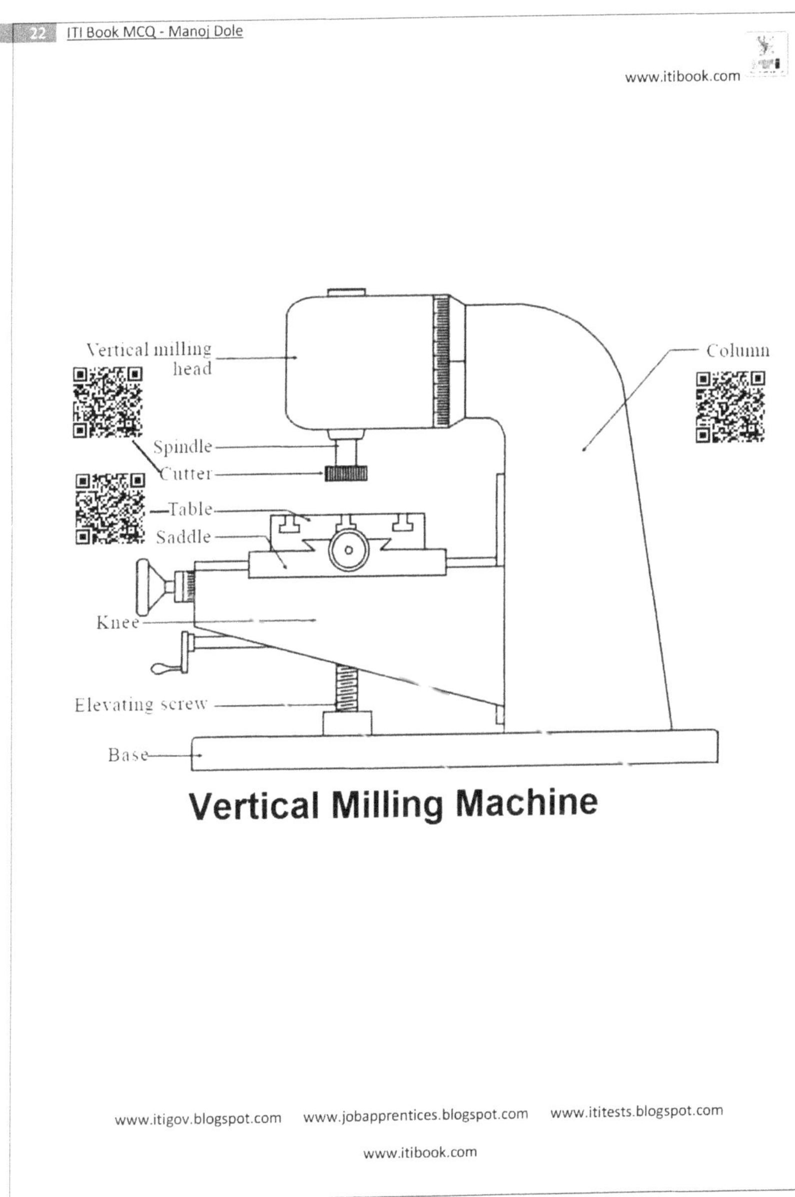

Vertical Milling Machine

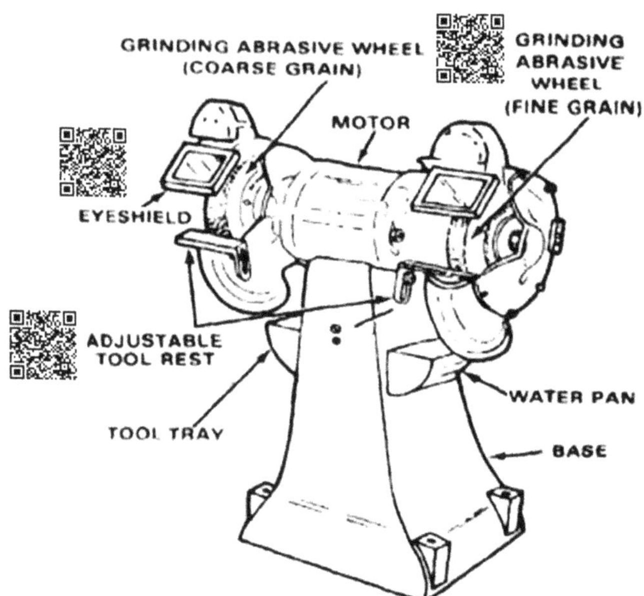

Pedastal Grinding Machine

www.itigov.blogspot.com www.jobapprentices.blogspot.com www.ititests.blogspot.com

www.itibook.com

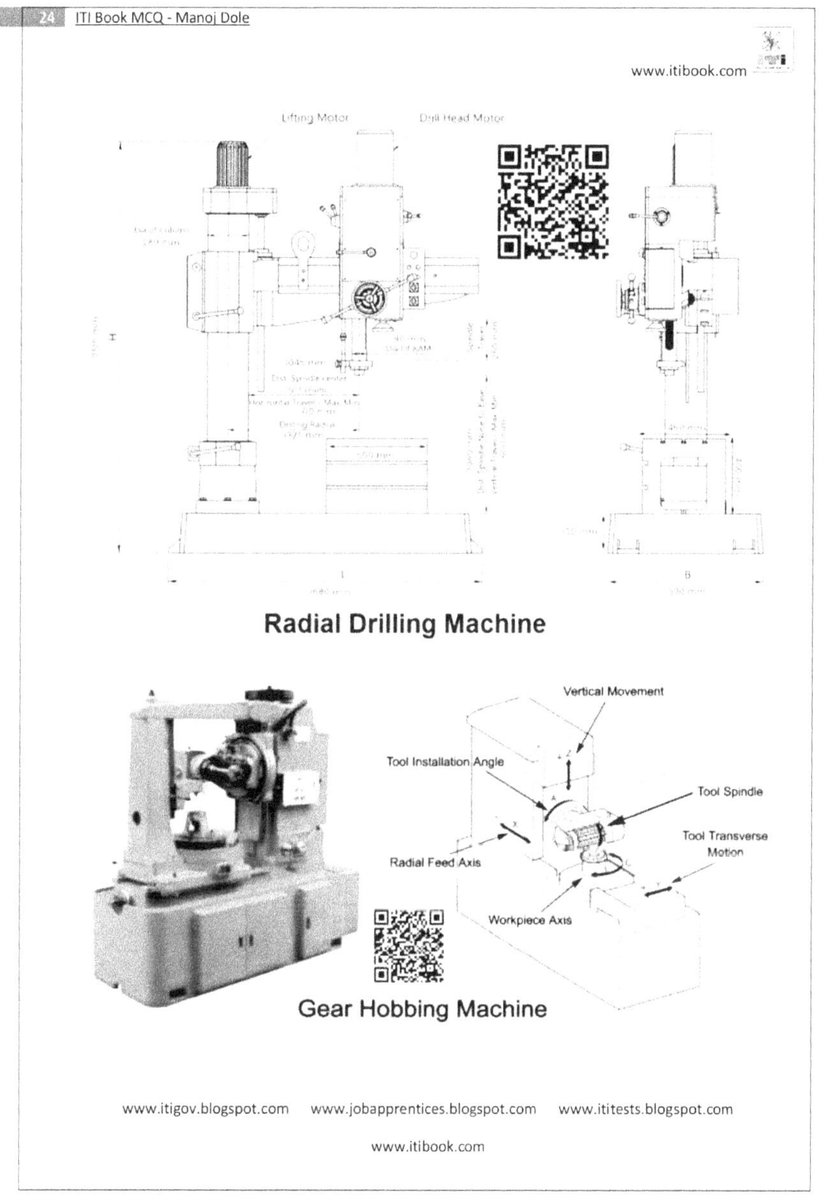

Radial Drilling Machine

Gear Hobbing Machine

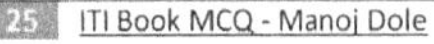

DOUBLE HOUSING PLANER

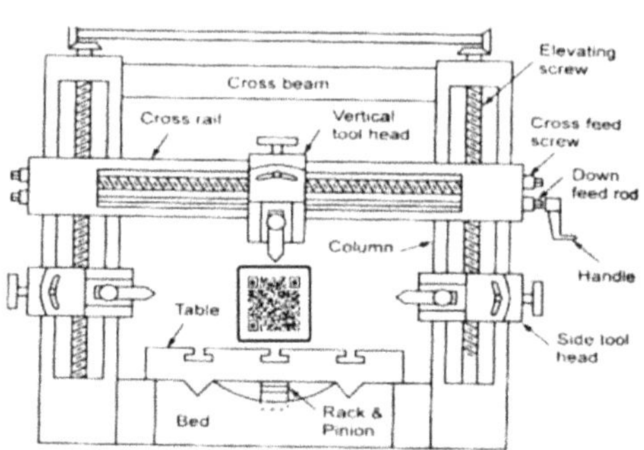

PIT PLANER

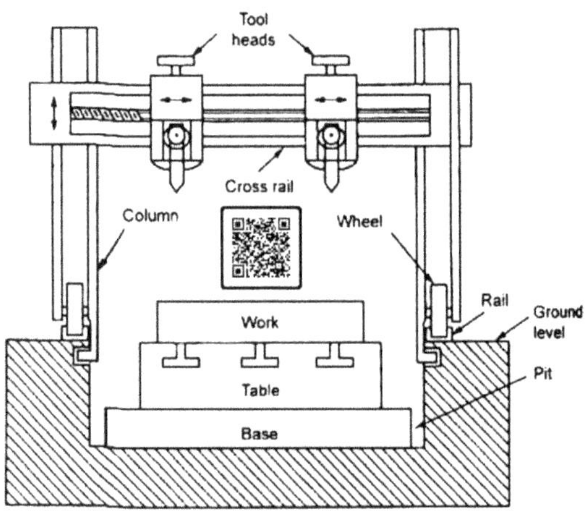

www.itibook.com

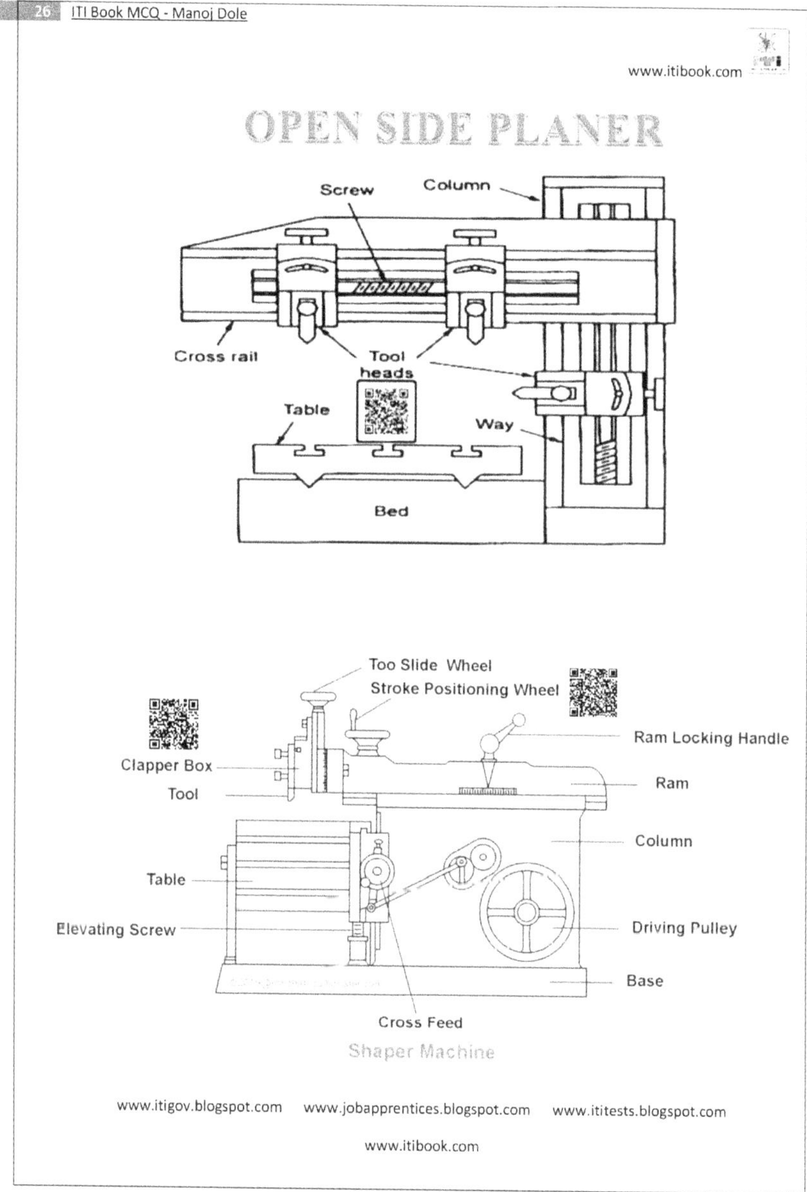

Shaper Machine

www.itigov.blogspot.com www.jobapprentices.blogspot.com www.ititests.blogspot.com

www.itibook.com

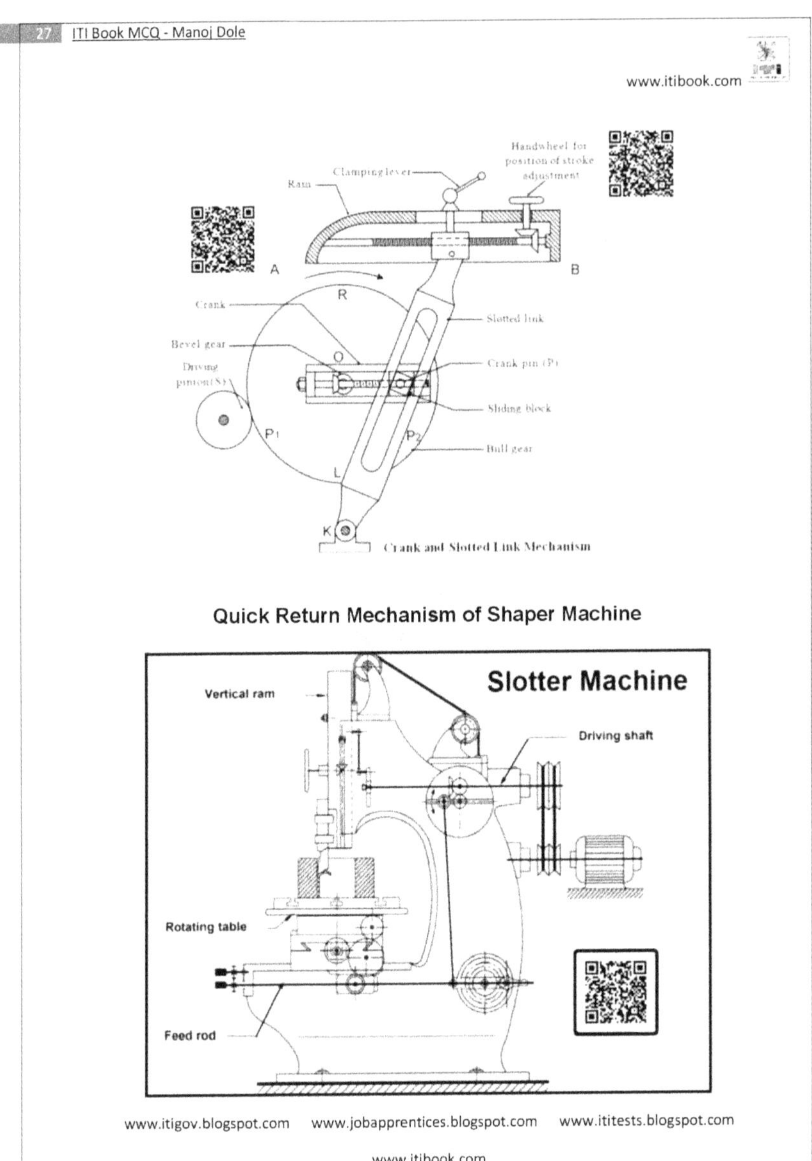
27 ITI Book MCQ - Manoj Dole
www.itibook.com
Handwheel for position of stroke adjustment
Clamping lever
Ram
A
B
R
Crank
Bevel gear
Driving pinion(S)
O
Slotted link
Crank pin (P)
Sliding block
P1
P2
Bull gear
L
K
Crank and Slotted Link Mechanism
Quick Return Mechanism of Shaper Machine
Slotter Machine
Vertical ram
Driving shaft
Rotating table
Feed rod
www.itigov.blogspot.com
www.jobapprentices.blogspot.com
www.ititests.blogspot.com
www.itibook.com

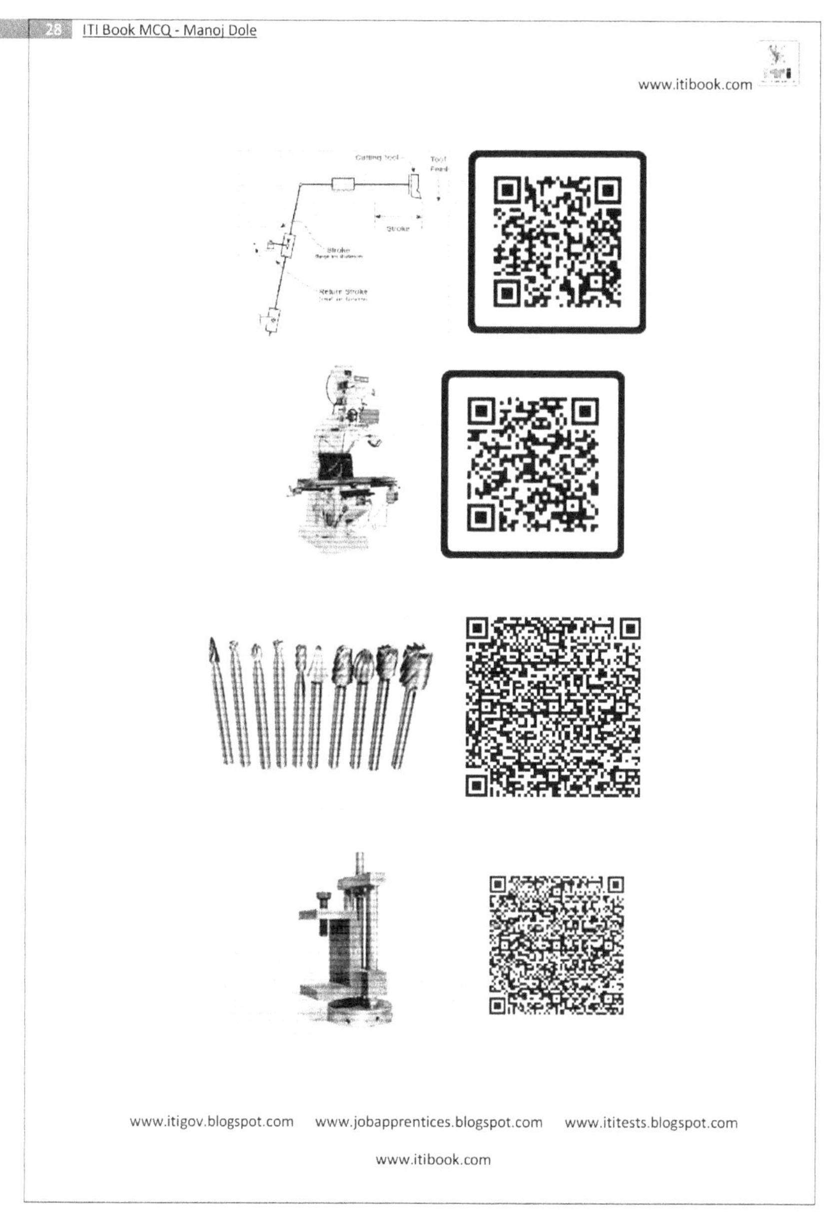

www.itibook.com

www.itigov.blogspot.com www.jobapprentices.blogspot.com www.ititests.blogspot.com

www.itibook.com

Machinist First Year MCQ

01] In Japanese Seiko stands for --------------

A] Shine

B] Sort

C] Standardize

D] Sustain

02] Benefit of SS system is ------

A] Increase in productivity

B] Increase in quality

C] Reduction in wastage of time

D] All of these

03] Safety is -----------

A] nobody's business

B] every bodise business

C] Some bodies business

D] The organization business

04] For basic categories of safety signs are available The meaning of"prohibition" sign ----

A] shows it must not be done

B] Shows what must be done

C] Warns the hazard or danger

D] Gives information of safety provision

05] In case of bleeding, take treatment Of

D] cold 3" and rest

A] spray cold water

B] Bandage immediately -----]

B] Enquire about the accident thought treatment

06] in case of an accident, the victim should im

A] Asked to take rest

C] Attended immediately

D] leave him

07] First aid is given to an injured or ill person primarily

A] Save life

B] Prevent further deterioration of the muff's

C] Give best possible comfort

D] All of these

08] Colour code for Bins for waste paper segregation is -----

A] blue Colour

B] Yellow Colour

C] Red Colour

D] Green Colour

09] Which one is a workshop safety?

A] Keep shop floor clean and free from grease, oil or other slippery materials

B] Stop the machine before changing the speed

C] Don't use cracked or chipped tools

D] Don't try to stop a running machine with hand

10] In Personal Protect Equipment (PPE] HELMET is used to

A] protect head

B] Protect eyes

C] Protect hands

D] Protect ears

11] Which of the following belongs to general safety?

A Have a worker in good attitude

B] The work clean and clear

C] Concentrate on your work

D] Keep the floor and gangways clean and clear

12] While grinding, which is used to protect the eyes?

A] Dark green glass

B] Mask

C] Sun glasses

D] Safety goggles

13] Which of the following is done for machine safety?

A] Check the oil level before starting the machine

B] Do things in a methodical way

C] Keep the floor and gangways clean and clear

D] Don't use dies and scarves

14] ln Personal Protect Equipment (PPE., 'sleeves' is used to protect ----------

A] Face

B] Eyes

C] Ears

D] Hands

15] ABC stands for --------------

A] Automatic Breathing Control

B] Automatic Blood Control

C] Airway Breathing Circulation

D] Automatic Blood Circulation

04] Fire & FIRE EXTINGUISHERS

16] To put off"Class B" fire, the types of fire extinguisher used is ....]

A] dry power

B] Carbon dioxide

C] Jet of water

D] Foam type

fire extinguisher Animation Videos

17] Which type of fire extinguisher is used to put off general fire?

A] Water type Extinguisher

B] Foam type Extinguisher

C] Dry chemical powder Extinguisher

D] Carbon dioxide (C02] Extinguisher

Hand tools & Measuring Instruments

18] One micrometer (U] is equal to...

A] 0.1mm

B] 0.01mm

C] 0.001mm

D] 0.0001mm

19] The caliper meant for measuring the width of a slot is...

A] Odd leg caliper

B] Outside caliper

C] Jenny caliper

D] Inside calliper

20] The size of the dividers are specified by the ----------

A] Total length of legs

B] Distance between the points when fully opened

C] Length of legs without points

D] distance between the pivot and the point

21] The instrument used to mark parallel lines, parallel to the datum edge is -

A] jenny caliper

B] Divider

C] Outside calliper

D] Inside calliper

22] Which one of the following is an indirect measuring tool?

A] Outside caliper

B] Vernier calliper

C] Steel rule

D] Outside micrometer

23] For cutting thin tubing, the most suitable pitch of the hacksaw blade is...

A] 1.8mm

B] 1.4mm

C] 1mm

D] 0.8mm

24] For cutting solid brass, the most suitable pitch of the hacksaw blade is...

A] 1.8mm

B] 1.4mm

C] 1mm

D] 0.8mm

25] A new hacksaw blade after a few strokes becomes loose because of the...

A] Stretching of the blade

B] Wing-nut threads being worn out

C] Wrong pitch of the blade

D] Improper selection of the set of saws.

26] While cutting small diameter pipes, it is advisable to watch regularly and ensure that...

A] The cut is along the curved line

B] More saw teeth are in contract

C] The work is not overheated

D] Proper balancing of hacksaw is maintained

27] The vice clamps are used to

A] Protect hard jaws

B] Clamp the work pieces rigidly

C] Protect the finished surfaces

D] Prevent the movable jaw being filed

28] The reference surface during marking is provided by the...

A] Surface gauge

B] Workpiece

C] Drawing of the work

D] Marking table surface

29] The size of an engineer's vice is specified by the

A] Length of the movable jaw

B] Width of the jaws

C] Height of the vice

D] Maximum opening of the jaws

30] The part of the universal surface gauge which helps to draw a parallel line along a datum edge is the..

A] Rocker arm

B] Snug

C] Fine adjustment screw

D] Guide pins

31] Scribers are made of...

A] Mild steel

B] High carbon steel

C] Brass

D] Cast iron

32] Portion of the hammer used for fixing the handle is

A] Face

B] Peen

C] Cheek

D] Eye hole

33] Weight of the hammer for the marking purpose is

A] 250g

B] 500g

C] 1 kg

D] 2 kgs

34] The size of the dividers are specified by the

A] Total length of the legs

B] Distance between the points when fully opened

C] Length of legs without the points

D] <u>Distance between the pivot and the point</u>

35] The included angle of the groove of 'V' block is always....

A] 45◦

B] 60◦

C] 90◦

D] <u>120◦</u>

36] 'V' blocks are available in grades of...

A] <u>A & B</u>

B] A,B & C

C] 1,2 & 3

D] 1 & 2

37] 'V' blocks of grade 'B' are made of

A] <u>Cast iron</u>

B] Mild steel

C] Steel

D] Cast steel

38] Name the punch used to locate the centre

A] Prick punch 30°

B] Prick punch 60°

C] Centre punch

D] Dot punch

39] The point angle of centre punch is --------

A] 30°

B] 50°

c] 900

D] 1200

40] Punches are used for forming ---------of any shape

A] Holes

B] Mining

C] Knurling

D] Reaming

41] Generally the length of the handle of the vice is ----------

A] 1.5 times the normal size of the vice

<u>B] 2.5 times the normal size of the vice</u>

C] 3.5 times the normal size of the vice

D] 4.5 times the normal size of the vice

42] Bench vice spindle is made of

<u>A] mild steel</u>

B] Cast iron

C] Tool steel

D] Bronze

<u>Types of Files</u>

43] The convexity of files helps

A] To file concave surfaces

B] To file convex surfaces

C] <u>To prevent rounding of edges of work</u>

D] The file to become straight when pressure is applied

44] Which file used for filling wood, leather and other soft material?]

A] Single cut file

B] Double cut file

<u>c] Rasp cut file</u>

D] Curved cut file

45] File used is used for ------------

A] Cleaning the work piece

C] Renewing the file teeth

<u>B] cleaning the file teeth</u>

D] Cleaning the chips

46] File card is used to --------

A] Clean the work piece

C] Renew the file teeth

B] Clean the file teeth

47] The point angle of scriber is ----------

A] 30°

B] 60°

C] 5° to 10°

D] 12° to 15°

48] The cutting angle for chipping cast iron is...

A] 37.5°

B] 55°

C] 60°

D] 90°

49] The chisel will dig into the material when...

A] The rake angle is more

B] The clearance angle is too low

C] The angle of inclination is more

D] The angle of inclination is too low

50] A slight convexity is given to the cutting edge to...

A] Cut curved surfaces

B] Cut sharp corners

C] <u>Prevent digging of the ends</u>

D] Allow the lubricant to enter

<u>Grinding & grinding wheel</u>

51] Aluminium oxide wheel is used for grinding ------------

A] cast iron

B] Cemented carbide.

C] <u>HSS ‘</u>

D] ceramic

52] The bond of diamond wheel suitable for offhand grinding of the tipped tool is

A] Resinoid

B] Vitrified

C] Shellac

<u>D] Metal</u>

53] Which among the following bonds, is used commonly?

<u>A] Vitrified bond ’</u>

B] Rubber bond

C] Shellac bond

D] Silicate bond

54] The symbol conventionally used for resinoid .bond is ~~~~~~~~

A] v

B] R f

C] B

D] E

55] In grinding practice the term "grade of wheel" refers to ---------‘

A] Hardness of the abrasive used

B] Strength of the bond of the wheel

C] Finish 0f the Wheel

D] Hardness of the work pieces

56] Which bond is used in cut of wheels?

A] Rubber

B] Vitrified

C] Resirjoid

D] Shellac

57] Grinding wheels made out of----------------- abrasive are most common because of its free and cool cutting action]

A] Aluminium oxide

B] Silicon oxide

C] Ammonium oxide

D] Carbide]

58] Which among the following abrasive is mostly used for cutting off wheels for cutting non metallic materials?

A] Aluminium oxide

B] Silicon carbide

C] Diamond

D] None of above

59] Which abrasive particle is used for grinding tungsten carbide tool insert?

A] Silicon carbide

B] A|203

C] Diamond

D] Corundum

60] Which of the following is the natural abrasive?

A] Aluminium oxide

B] Silicon

C] Boron carbide

D] Corundum

61] Which of the following is the manufactured abrasive?

A] Corundum]

B] Quartz

C] Silicon

D] Emery

62] Which abrasive particle is used for grinding steel fittings?

A] Silicon carbide

B] Aluminium oxide

C] Diamond]

D] boron oxide

63] What kind of abrasive cut of wheel should be used to cut concrete stone and masonry?

A] Silicon

B] Al203

C] Diamond grit

D] Glass

64] Hardness of grinding wheel is determine by ----------

A] the resistance exerted] by the bond against grinding Stress

B] Hardness of abrasive grains

C] Hardness of bond

D] Ability to penetration

65] When it is required to run a Grinding wheel safely at very high speed, which bond should be used? "

A] Vitrified

B] Shellac

C] Silicate

<u>D] resinoid' and rubber</u>

66] in surface grinding what is the suitable range of grain size of the grinding wheel for general purpose surface grinding?

A] 20 to 36

<u>B] 46 to 60</u>

C] 80 to 120

D] 150 to 300

67] AS per Indian Standard, the grain '46'.comes under the group of «w] -----

A] Coarse

<u>B] Medium</u>

C] Fine

D] Very fine

68] The grit size of the abrasives used in the grinding wheel is usually specified by ----------

A] Hardness number

B] A size of wheel

C] Softness or hardness of the abrasive

D] Mesh number

69] Bench grinder are used for

A] Heavy duty work

B] Heavy and light duty work

C] Light duty work

D] Lather work

70] Bench Grinders are fitted on a

A] Base

B] Table]

C] Wheel guards

D] Conveyor

Drilling & Drill chuck

71] The taper shank drills are held on the machine by means of...

A] Chucks

B] Sleeves

C] Drift

D] Vice

72] Drill chucks are fitted on the drilling machine spindle by means of a...

A] Knurled ring

B] Arbor

C] Drift

D] Pinion and key

73] The Morse taper provided on drills ranges between

A] MT 1 to MT 5

B] MT 1 to MT 4

C] MT 0 to MT 5

D] MT 0 to MT 4

74] A drift is used for...

A] Drawing a drill location

B] Fixing chuck on the machine spindle

C] Removing a broken drill from the work

D] Removing the drill from the machine spindle

75] When the taper shank of the drill is larger than the machine spindle, the device to hold the drill is a...

A] Drill sleeve

B] Taper socket

C] Drill drift

D] Chuck and key

76] The suitable cutting fluid for drilling mild steel in a drilling machine is...

A] Synthetic soluble oil

B] Neat oil

C] Distilled water

D] Soluble oil

77] A special feature of the radial drilling machine is

A] It can be used for drilling with a H.S.S] drill

B] Table can be moved and set at any position

C] A variety of speeds is available

D] The spindle can be brought to any position

78] The point angle of drills depends on

A] The size of the drill

B] The type of machine

C] The material of the work

D] The RPM of the drill

79] The point angle for a standard drill is

A] 60◦

B] 108◦

C] 118◦

D] 135◦

80] The helical angle determines the

A] Cutting angle

B] Chew angle

C] Rake angle

D] Lip angle

81] The clearance angle of the drill is between

A] 3◦ to 5◦

B] 8◦ to 12◦

C] 12◦ to 20◦

D] 15◦ to 20◦

82] In a remote place (no electricity available] a rail track is to be drilled] Choose the right drilling machine

A] Radial drilling machine

B] Pillar drilling machine

C] Ratchet drilling machine

D] Sensitive drilling Machine

83] A drilling machine used by a carpenter for cabinet making is a

A] Ratchet drilling machine

B] Radial drilling machine

C] Breast drilling machine

D] Sensitive drilling machine

84] Which one of the following drilling machines is used for drilling holes where electricity is not available?

A] Bench drilling machine

B] Pillar drilling machine

C] Redial drilling machine

D] Ratchet drilling machine

85] Which one of the following drilling machine is used for heavy duty work?

A] Bench drilling machine

B] Pillar drilling machine

C] Radial drilling machine

D] Electric hand drilling machine

86] Drill chuck are held on the machine spindle by means of ------

A] arbor

B] Drift

C] draw-in bar

D] Chuck nut

87] Different speeds are obtained in a sensitive bench drilling machine by ----

A] Belt pulley mechanism

B] Hydraulic mechanism

C] Rack and Pinion mechanism

D] Cam and follower mechanism

Tap & Dies

88] The tapping drill size for M10 x 15 is ----------

A] 8.2

B] 8.3

C] 8.4

D] 8.5

89] A nut is to be made for a screw of M10XI.S] What should be the size of drilled hole?

A] 8-5 mm

B] 9.0 mm

C] 9.5 mm

D] 10.0 mm

90] Tap are re-sharpened by grinding

A] Flutes

B] Threads

C] Diameter

D] Relief

91] Which size drill is used for taping width MS tap?

A] 4.5 mm

B] 4.0 mm

C] 0.38mm

D] 0.35mm

92] Which one of the following is used to operate form of thread by hand?

A} Tap

B] Threading tool

C] Threading chaser

D] Tipped tool

93] In hand tapping operation, no of taps used are ----

A] 2

B] 3

C] 4

D] 5

94] To get 100% tap in a hole the size of the hole must be equal to ----

A] Minor diameter of the tap

B] Intermediate diameter of the tap

C] Major diameter of the tap

D] None of these

95] A die in which more than one cutting operation is per formed in one stroke

A] Piercing die

B] Progressive die

C] Combination die

D] Compound die

96] A die in which cutting and non cutting operations are carried out per stroke.

A] Piercing die

B] Progressive die

C] Combination die

D] Compound die

97] A die in which two or more sequential operations are performed at two or more stations upon the work.

A] Piercing die

B] Progressive die

C] Combination die

D] Compound die

98] A die in which the shape of the punch and die are directly reproduced in the metal with little or no metal flow.

A] Progressive die

B] Combination die

C] Compound die

D] Forming die

99] The die used for producing any shape of holes.

A] Piercing dic

B] Progressivc die

C] Combination die

D] Compound die

100] A short reamer with an axial hole used with an arbor or mandrel is called -------

A] Parallel reamer

B] Adjustable reamer

C] Expansion reamer

D] Chucking reamer

101] Which one of the following machine reamers is used to correct the misalignment between the reamer axis and the work axis?

A] Floating blade reamer

B] Machine jig reamer]

C] Shell reamer

D] Chucking reamer

vernier height gauge

102] The least count of a vernier height gauge in the metric system is

A] 0.05 mm

B] 0.1 mm

C] 0.02 mm

D] 0.001 mm

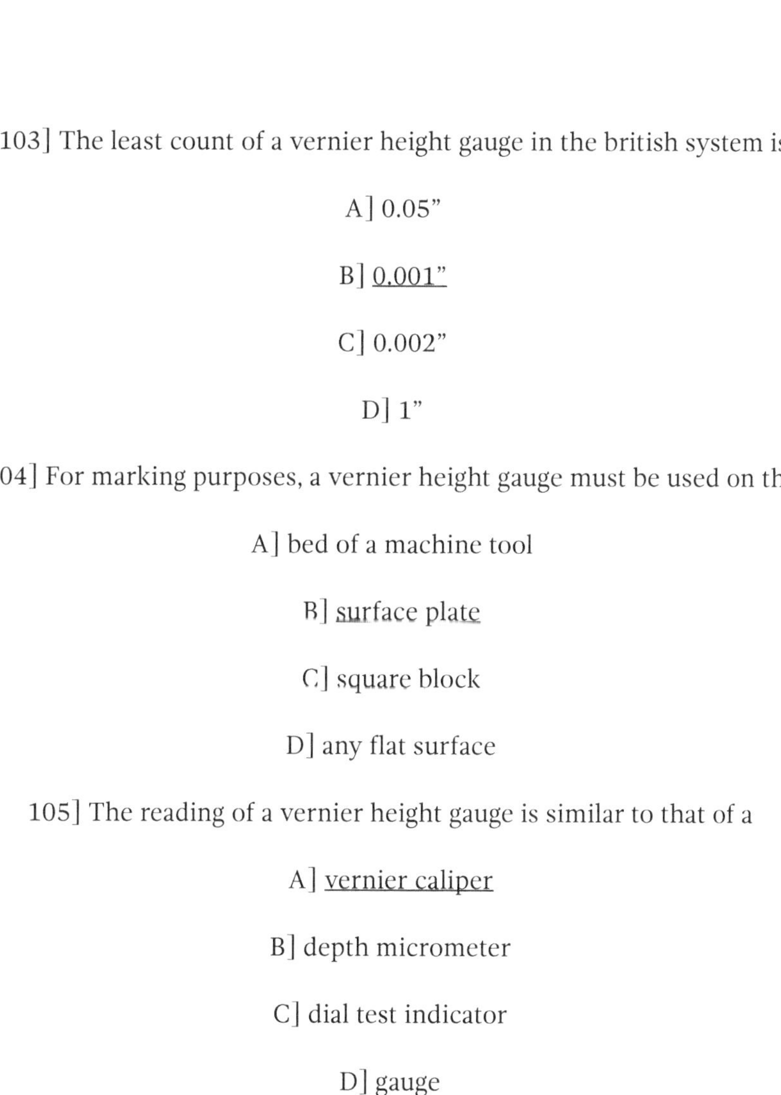

103] The least count of a vernier height gauge in the british system is

A] 0.05”

B] 0.001”

C] 0.002”

D] 1”

104] For marking purposes, a vernier height gauge must be used on the

A] bed of a machine tool

B] surface plate

C] square block

D] any flat surface

105] The reading of a vernier height gauge is similar to that of a

A] vernier caliper

B] depth micrometer

C] dial test indicator

D] gauge

106] The part which slides on the beam of a vernier height gauge is known as a

A] base

B] beam scale

C] scriber

D] vernier slide

107] The size of a vernier height gauge is specified by the

A] height of the vernier scale

B] height of the beam

C] width of the beam

D] size of the base

108] The base of the vernier height gauge is generally made out of

A] cast iron

B] steel

C] aluminium alloy

D] tungsten carbide

Limits and fits

109] In the BIS system of limits and fits, the grade of tolerance are represented by number Symbols and there are ---------i

A] 14 grades of tolerance

B] 16 grades of tolerance

C] 18 grades of tolerance '

D] 20 grades of tolerance

110] A Product is said to have the quality when

A] Its shape and dimensions are within the limit

B] It is fit for use

C] It appears to be very good

D] The choice of material is right

111] The maximum clearance required between hole'30 +0..021, 0.000 and shaft 30 -0.110, 0.143 is.

A] 0.110 mm '

B.0.131 mm

C] 0.164 mm

D] 0.143 mm

112] A dimension is stated as 25 .1002 mm in a drawing] What is the tolerance?

A] +0.02 mm'

B] +0.04 mm

C] -0.02 mm

D] 25.00 mm

113] A pin is fitted in a hole] The tolerance zone of the pin is entirely above that of hole] The fit obtained will be?

A] Clearance fit

B] Transition fit

C] Interference fit

D] Running fit

114] Tolerance is given to the part size to

A] Production the part within the required permissible size error

B] Increase the production

C] Decrease the Production

D] Finish the components approximately

115] Which one of the following is the clearance fit under the whole basic system?

A] 20 H7/p6'

B] 2067/211

C] ZOG/gll

D] 20H/g11

116] The three classes of fits as per BIS system aré

A] Clearance fit, interference fit and transition fit

B] Medium fit, push fit and tight fit

C] Flat fit, round fit and square fit

D] 'Sliding fit ', loose fit and shrinkage fit

117] Which one of the following tolerance specifications has a maximum dimensionless than 20 mm?

A] 20 +0.2,-0.3

B] 20 320.2

C] 20 -0.2, 0.3 e

D.m 20 +500, ~03

118] Difference between the maximum and minimum limit is --------------------

A] Single informant

B] Basic shaft

C] Clearance

D] Tolerance

119] A shaft 55 running freely in bush bearing the type of fit is ---------

A] Clearance fit

B] Driving plate

C] shrinkage fit

D] None of the above

120] The least count of vernier calliper is (main scale = 49 division, vernier scale = 50 division]

A] 0.1 mm

B] 0.01 mm

C] 0.001 mm

<u>D] 0.02 mm</u>

121] The type of measurement made by using a Vernier Calliper is -------

A] Direct measurement

<u>B] Indirect measurement</u>

C] 90“] (a] 81 (b]

D] None of these

<u>Outside micrometer</u>

122] in a metric micrometer, a complete revolution of thimble advances -----------

A] 0.01 mm

B] 0.25 mm

C] 0.50 mm

D] 1.00mm

123] Ratchet Stop in the micrometer helps to ------------

A] Control the pressure

B] lock the spindle

C] Adjust the zero error

D] Hold the work piece

124] 1000 micron means ------------

A] 1 mm

B] 1 m

C] 1000 mm

D] 10 cm

125] What is the zero reading of a 50-75 mm outside micrometer?

A] 0.000 mm

B] 0.01 mm

C] 25.00 mm

D] 50.00 mm

126] The value of the smallest division on sleeve of a metric outside micrometer is -----

A] 0.50 mm

B] 1.00 mm

C] 1.50 mm

D] 2.00 mm

127] Ratchet stop in the micrometer helps to ---------

A] control the pressure

B] Lock the spindle

C] Adjust the zero error

D] Hold the work piece

128} Uses of a dial test indicator are ----------

A] To check plane surface for parallelism and flatness

B] To check the straightness of shaft and bars

C] To check concentricity of holes and shafts

D] All the above

129] The dial test indicators shows that the measurement as -------

A] The magnified small variation is size through a point

B] The difference between the top steps of the 5 mm

C] The actual size of the component

D] The direct reading of the dimension

130] Name the instrument which magnifies the small variation is size measured]

A] Vernier calliper

B] Micrometer

C] Dial indicator

D] Steel rule

131] The cutting speed for aluminium with H.S.S] tools is

A.] 30 m/min

B.] 50 m/min

C.] 70 m/min

D.] 130 m/min

132] The cutting speed for brass with a H.S.S] tool is

A.] 10 m/min

B.] 25 m/min

C.] 70 m/min

D.] 140 m/min

133] The depth of cut for M24 x 3 mm internal thread is

A] 0.5412 x 3

B] 0.6134 x 3

C] 0.5 x 3

D] 0.7 x 3

134] To cut 24 x 3 mm internal acme threads, the core diameter of the job is

A] 20.00 mm

B] 21.66 mm

C] 21.00 mm

D] 20.60 mm

135] The depth of cut for metric square threading is

A] 0.6 x P

B] 0.5 x P

C] 0.5412 x P

D] 0.6412 x P

136] To cut buttress thread, the depth of cut is

A] 0.5412 x P

B] 0.6 x P

C] 0.7 x P

D] 0.75 x P

Types of Lathe

137] How many types of Lathe as per manufacturing?

A] Two

B] Three

C] Four

D] Five

138] How many types of Centre Lathe?

A] Two

B] Three

C] Four

D] Five

139] How many types of production lathe?

A] Two

B] Three

C] Four

D] Five

140] Which type of lathe is Roller Lathe?

A] Bench Lathe

B] Special Lathe

C] Production Lathe

D] Centre Lathe

141] For mass-production which machine is used?

A] Centre Lathe

<u>B] Production Lathe</u>

C] Special Lathe

D] Engine Lathe

142] Which lathe is used for more accurate job?

A] Centre Lathe

B] Special Lathe

C] Production Lathe

<u>D] Tool Room Lathe</u>

143] The accuracy of Tool Room Lathe is to Compeer Centre Lathe.]

(A] Less

<u>(B] More</u>

(C] Very Less

(D] Equal

144] In Locomotive Assemble Wheel with Axel is turning on Lathe

(A] Centre Lathe

(B] Tool Room Lathe

<u>(C] Wheel Lathe</u>

(D] Gap Bed Lathe

145] Cast iron is used for manufacturing machine beds because -------

<u>A] it can resist more compressive stress</u>

B] it is heavy in weight

C] It is cheaper metal

D] It is a brittle metal

146] Which one of the following operations can't be performed on a Center Lathe?]

A] Turning

B] Thread cutting

<u>C] Gear cutting</u>

D] Taper turning

147] The cutting edge of a solid tool is made of

A] <u>carbon steel</u>

B] mild steel

C] super high speed steel

D] stelite

148] The tip of a cemented carbide threading tool is

A] brazed

B] welded

C] soldered

D] clamped to the shank

149] Tool will rub against the work surfaces and the cutting force increases when..

A] The clearance angle is more

B] The clearance angel is less

C] The rake angle is more

D] The rake angle is less

150] Formation of a chip while cutting is based on the...

A] Rake angle of the tool

B] Clearance angle of the tool

C] Wedge angle of the tool

D] Clearance and wedge angle of the tool

151] in following drawing, which of the front clearance angel?

A] Front clearance angle

B] Wedge angle

C] Cutting angle

D] Back rake angle

152] When cutting tool start his action & cutting force in increase at this position subsequent effect of tool is..?

A] Clearance angle of tool is high

B] Clearance angle of tool is low

C] Rake angle of tool is low

D] Rake angle of tool is high

153] The purpose of Rake angle for tool is?

A] Right direction for mental chips

B] Good finishing on job

C] For increase life of tool

D] For avoid friction in between job & tool

154] The purpose of provide clearance angle for cutting tool is?

A] For right direction of metal cutting chips

B] reduce friction on hit of job

C] for sage of job friction

D] for better finishing on job

155] If cutting tools setting upper centre height done what happen?

A] Encrease top Rake angle

B] less top Rake angle

C] No effect on Top Rake angle

D] Encrease clearance angle

156] What happen if cutting tool setting done lower of center height?

A] Encrease top Rake angle

B] Decrease top Rake angle

C] No any effect on to Rake

D] Decrease clearance angle

157] If cutting tool is upsetting of centre of job?

A] Encrease front clearance angle

B] Decrease front clearance angle

C] no any effect on front clearance angle

D] none of them

158] If cutting tool is down setting of centre of job?

A] Front clearance angle is increase

B] Front clearance angle is decrease

C] No any effect on clearance angle

D] None of them

159] Zero Rake angle give for tool?

A] To avoid friction of tool

B] For increase tool life

C] For increase straight of tool

D] For better finishing on job

160] For carbide tip tool turning on hard material it has……essential?

A] Side Rake angle

B] Zero Rake angle

C] Positive Rake angle

D] Negative Rake angle

161] For do not break cutting edge of cutting tool…?

A] Feed increase

B] Cutting speed done low

C] Length of nose decrease

D] Use negative rake angle

162] Chip breaker in a tool is given

A] 'It break the chips into small pieces

B] to have continuous type of chips from long cut

C] to have crushed chips]

163] Step type chip breaker is the one

A] in which a small groove is ground behind the cutting edge

B] in which a step IS ground on the face of the tool along the cutting edge

C] in which a thin carbide plate or clamp is brazed or screwed on the face of the tool]

164] For mounting a lathe chuck

A] start it by hand and then turn the power on

B] mount it on by power

C] mount it by hand

D] mount it with the help of a hammer

165] The least count of a vernier bevel protractor is...

A] 1”

B] 5’

C] 1◦

D] 5 ◦

166] The part of a vernier bevel protractor which is normally used as a reference base for measuring angles is the...

A] Blade

B] Stock

C] Disc

C] Main scale

167] The part of a vernier bevel protector on which main scale divisions are marked is the...

A] Stock

B] Dial

C] Disc

D] Adjustable blade

168] The part of a bevel protractor, which comes in contact with the inclined surface while measuring is the...

A] Blade

B] Stock

C] Disc

D] Dial

169] The value of each division of the main scale of a vernier bevel protractor is...

A] 5’

B] 1◦

C] 5◦

D.10◦

170] The value of each division of the vernier scale of a bevel protractor is...

A] 1◦

B] 1◦5’

C] 1◦55’

D.5’

171] The part of the vernier bevel protractor on which main scale divisions are marked

A stock

B dial

C disc

D adjustable blade

172] In Vernier bevel protractor is designed to measure?

A] Acute angles

B] Obtuse angles

C] Acute and Obtuse angle

D] Liner dimensions

173] To get least count of 5 in a vernier bevel protractor the 23° main scale are divided into -..

A] 12 equal parts on vernier scale

B] 22 equal parts on vernier scale

C] 24 equal parts on vernier scale

D] 25 equal parts on vernier scale

174] The process of enlarging the end of a hole for accommodating the socket screw head is...

A] Reaming

B] Spot facing

C] Counter boring

D] Counter sinking

175.While choosing a boring tool for boring a given diameter, select

A] a long tool

B] a short tool

C] a long and stout tool

D] a short and stout tool

176] The cutting edge of the boring tool should be set for a small hole so that it is

A] 0.5 mm above the center

B] 0.5 mm below the center

C] 1 mm above the center

D] in the exact center

177] Bored holes are to be chamfered by using

A] a drill

B] triangular scraper

C] a cranked boring tool

D] a flat file

178] The tool used for boring deep holes is a

A] Sleeve

B] Drill

C] Boring bar

D] Auger bit

179] The cutting speed for rough boring is the

A] same as rough turning

B] same as drilling

C] same as knurling

D] same as thread cutting

180] Knurling operation is done at the

A] turning spindle speed

B] high spindle speed

C] 1/3 of the turning spindle speed

D] 1/2 of the turning spindle speed

181] Knurling is the operation of

A] shearing

B] forming

C] turning

D] pressing

182] The taper ratio of the morse taper is

A] 1 in 10

B] 1 in 15

C] 1 in 20

D] 1 in 25

183] The morse standard taper is available in

A] 16 Nos

B] 12 Nos

C] 10 Nos

D] 8 Nos

184] Taper turning by offsetting the tailstock method can produce

A] an internal taper

B] an internal taper thread

C] an external taper

D] both external and internal tapers

185] By using the taper turning attachment, tapers can be turned with a setting angle up to

A] 10°

B] 15°

C] 20°

D] 30°

186] The accuracy of a taper is generally checked by means of.

A] taper gauges

B] gauge blocks

C] indicator and height gauge

D] 'V' blocks

187] Turning tapers by the compound rest method involves working solely with

A] Decimal measurements

B] fractional measurements

C] metric measurements

D] angular measurements]

188] Long tapers are produced

A] with the taper turning attachment

B] with the compound slide

C] by setting over the tail stock

D] by adjusting the cross slide]

189] The length of turned tapers are checked with

A] vernier calliper

B] micrometer

C] inside callper

D] dial test indicator]

190] The disadvantages of taper turning using the com] pound slide are

A] only long tapers can be turned

B] only very large tapers can be turned

C] only manual in feed is possible

D] only short tapers can be turned due to the restrictions of the compound slide]

191] External tapers are checked with

A] limit plug gauge

B] taper ring gauge

C .taper plug gauge

D] thread plug gauge]

192] The use of a taper turned on lathe is ----

A] Assist to transmit drive in the assembled parts

B] Used for Assembly and disassembly of parts

C] Give self alignment in the assembled parts

193] Which type of method is used in mass production of production of producing small length of taper?

A] Form tool

B] Compound slide

C] Tailstock offset.

D] Taper turning attachment

194] Morse standard taper is one of the internationally accepted standards taper, which is available in numbers from--------

A.1to7

B.1 to 8

C] O to 7

D] 0 to 8

195] Which taper turning method is used for cutting steep taper?

A] Set over method

B] Taper turning attachment

C] Form tool

D] Swivelling the compound rest

196] Morse taper is used in which of the following machine components -...

A] Spindles of lathe

B] Spindles of drill machine

C] Shanks of reamers

D] All of these

197] For mass production of the taper which one of the following method is used]

A] Tailstock offset method

B] Taper turning attachment method

C] Form too method

D] Compound slide method

198] The major diameter of the taper is 40 mm, minor diameter is 30 mm] The total length of the job is 100 mm is tapered then offset is given by -

A] 5 mm

B] 7.5 mm

C] 12 mm

D] 9 mm

Sine bar

199] Sine bar is made of

A] high carbon steel

B] high speed steel

C] nickel steel

D] stabilized chromium steel]

200] Sine bar is used for

A] levelling the job for drilling

B] finding the angle of taper job

C] measuring diameter of holes

D] checking profile of thread]

201] Length of sine bar is the distance between

A] one end to another end of sine bar

B] diagonal cross length of the sine bar

C] centre to centre between rollers

D] outside to outside between rollers]

202] The size of a sine bar is specified by it's

A] weight

B] measurement of width

C] length

D] maximum angle of setting]

203.The purpose of providing a stopper at one end of the sine bar is for

A] easy handling

B] preventing the job from slipping]

C] supporting the slip gauge

D] using as a reference while setting]

204] A sine bar is made with four or five equally'spaced holes on its body] The purpose of these holes is to

A] Handle the sine bar easily

B] Reduce the weight of sin bar

C] Prevent distortion of the top surface of sine bar

D] Give good appearance to the sine bar

205] A sine bar is used for

A] Measuring the diameter of holes '

B] Finding the angle of a taper job

C] Leveling the job for drilling

D] Chuckin'g the profile of a thread

206] For measuring angles using the sine bar the angle framed according to the ratio between the height of slip gauge and the

A] Height of sine bar

B] Number slip gauge

C] Length of sine bar

D] Width of sine bar

207] -----------is used for checking angle within an accuracy of 1

A] Gauge

B] Sine bar

C] Temple

D] Telescopic gauge

208] Centre line of the contact rollers and datum surface if the sine bar are

A] Same line' '

B] Parallel

C] Inclined

D] Perpendicular

209] The sine bar is made of .

A] High carbon steel

B] Stabilized chromium steel '

C] High speed steel

D] Nicked steel

210] A sine bar with a length of l=200mm is used to check accurately the angle of a Work piece] The angle to be checked: 250 calculate the height 'h' of the slip gauges?

A] 84.54mm

B] 83.52mm

C] 81.81mm

D] 85.52mm

211] Which of the following statement is correct?'

A] Gauges are used to check the size

B] Template are used to chuck-the size

C] Gauges are used to measure the size

D] Gauges are used to check shape of component

212] At what standard temperature are the gauges kept in the section?

A] 100 C

<u>B] 20° C</u>

C] 100 F

D] 20° F

213] Which grade of slip gauge is generally used in workshop?

A] Grade 0

B] Grade l

C] Grade H

<u>D] Grade 0</u>

<u>Slip Gauges</u>

214] As per Indian Standards a special set gauge is used consisting of

A] 81 Pieces

<u>B] 112 Pieces</u>

C] 120 Pieces

D] 130 Pieces

215] The accuracy of reference gauge is

A] 0.05 mm

B] 0.01 mm

C] 0.001]

D] 0.0001 mm

216] In case of ant burr on slip gauge, it should be removed by

A] Filling

B] Lapping

C] Scraping

D] Grinding

217] Hardness of slip gauge should be?

A] More than 63 HRC

B] 58 HRC

C] 55 HRC

D] 50 HRC

218.------------- Slip gauge is used for Checking component within an accuracy of 0.01 mm]

A] Workshop gauge

B] Inspection gauge

C] Reference gauge

D] Ring gauge

219., ------------is used for checking accuracy of precision instrument]

A] Gauge block

B] Fader gauge

C] Sine bar

D] Plug gauge

220] Slip gauge are Cleaned before using to ensure accuracy] What medium will you use for this purpose.

A] Oil

B] Thinner

C] Carbon tetrachloride/ White petrol

D] Turpentine oil

221 .To check the dimensional accuracy of identical components, a dial test indicator is set-for t 6 Size and used as a comparator] What will you use to set to the dial test indicator?

A] Dial test indicator

B] Teeter gauge

C] Slip gauge

D., surface gauge

222] which one of the following statement about Sine bar is not correct?

A] Uses tow precision rollers kept on either side

B] Made of the Chromium steel

C] The surface is lapped

D] The centrelines of the holes will be inclined to the top surface

223] A slip gauge is a ---------

A] Rectangular block

B] Square block

C] Cubic block

D] Cylindrical block

224] In 4th SERIES of slip gauge, which one of the following range is correct in set 46 pieces

A] 1.0 to 9.0 mm.

B] 1.001 101.009 mm

C] 1.01 to 1.09 mm

D.'1.1'to_-1.9mm

225] In 5th SERIES of slip gauge, which one Of the following range is correct in set 46 pieces –

A] 100 to 100 mm '

B] 1.001 to 1.009 mm

C] 1.01 to 0.09mrn

D] 11 to 9mm

226] In 2NDS SERIES of slip gauge, which one of the following range IS correct in set of 45 pieces-

A] 1.0 to 9.0 mm

B] 1.001 to 1] 009 mm

C] 1.01 to 1.09 mm

D] 1.1 to 1.9mm

227] In 3RD SERIES of slip gauge, which one of the following range is correct in set 46 pieces –

A] 10.0 to 100 mm

B] 1.001 to 1.009 mm

C] 1.01 to 1.09 mm

D] 1.1 to 1.9 mm

228] In 1ST SERIES of slip gauge, which one of the following range is correct in set 46 pieces –

A] 0.001mm

B] 001mm

C] 0.1mm

D] 1.0mm

229] In 2ned SERIES of slip gauge, which one of the following STEP is correct in set of 46 pieces –

A] 0.001mm

B] 0.01 mm

C] 0.1 mm

D] 1-0 mm

230] In 3rd SERIES of slip gauge, which one of the following STEP Is correct in set 46 pieces

A] 0.001mm

B] 0.01mm

C] 0.1 mm

D] 1.0mm

231] A BSW threading tool is to be ground with an included angle of

A] 55°

B] 60°

C] 47.5°

D] 29°

232] The nose radius of a metric 'V' thread tool is

A] 0.144 x P

B] 0.25 x P

C] 0.414 x P

D] 0.0144 x P

233] While cutting metric external threads of coarse pitches, it is advisable to swivel the compound rest to

A] 45◦

B] 30◦

C] 60◦

D.90◦

234] The depth of B.I.S] metric thread is

A] 0.6403 x P

B] 0.6 x P

C] 0.6134 x P

D] 0.5 x P

235] Threading tools are checked for accuracy for the 60◦ angle by using a

A] Thread plug gauge

B] centre gauge

C] screw pitch gauge

D] tool angle gauge

236] The number of threads per inch can be checked with a

A] tool gauge

B] metric rule by counting

C] ring gauge

D] screw pitch gauge

237] When threading, the carriage is moved along the ways by

A] a gear train on a track

B] the feed rod spline or key-way

C] the lead screw thred

D] the hand wheel

238] Thread chasers are used for

A] quick production of threads

B] maintaining an exact form of thread

C] cutting threads on hard materials

D] cutting threads on soft materials

239] Thread chasers are made out of

A] carbon steel

B] high speed steel

C] tool used

D] stainless steel

240] Chasers are used to cut

A] 'V' form threads only

B] square threads only

C] acme threads only

D] any form of threads

241] To cut M24 x 3 mm pitch internal threads, the core diameter of the job is

A] 27.00 mm

B] 24.50 mm

C] 21.00 mm

D] 24.00 mm

242] The depth of cut for M24 x 3 mm internal thread is

A] 0.5412 x 3

B] 0.6134 x 3

C] 0.5 x 3

D] 0.7 x 3

243] To cut 24 x 3 mm internal acme threads, the core diameter of the job is

A] 20.00 mm

B] 21.66 mm

C] 21.00 mm

D] 20.60 mm

244] The depth of cut for metric square threading is

A] 0.6 x P

B] 0.5 x P

C] 0.5412 x P

D] 0.6412 x P

245] To cut buttress thread, the depth of cut is

A] 0.5412 x P

B] 0.6 x P

C] 0.7 x P

D] 0.75 x P

246] For cutting acme threads, the tool is ground to an included angle of

A] 60°

B] 29°

C] 47.5°

D] 30°

247] The half-nut lever is used for

A] engaging the longitudinal feed on the carriage

B] taking up the slack in the cross-slide nut

C] changing from longitudinal to cross-feed

D] threads cutting

248] The bottom surface joining the two sides of adjacent thread (external thread] is...

A] Flank

B] Root

C] Crest

D] Pitch

249] The form of thread used in carpenters vice is...

A] Square

B] Acme thread

C] Sawtooth Thread

D] Knuckle thread

250] What is the angle of pipe thread?

A] 60°

B] 47‘/2°

C] 29°

D] 55°

251] What is the use of pipe thread?

A] transmission

B] maintain pressure

C] airtight connections

D] none of the above]

252] What is the depth of the 2" pipe thread?

A] 0.5"

B] 0.640“

C] 0.335"

D] 0.580"]

253] External Thread provide on Rod or Pipe , by Die and Cutting Tool is called .

(A] Tapping

(B] Dieing

(C] Threading

(D] Grooving

254] The angle 0f lS thread (V shaped] is ----------

A] 29°

B] 47 1/4°

C] 50°

D] 60

255] ln which of the following methods, only external threads are made -------

A] Form tool mEthOd

B] Compound rest method

C] Tailstock offset method

D] Taper turning attachment method]

256] The surface joining the crest and the root of a thread is known as ----

A] Flank

B] Shank

C] Pitch surface

D] All Of these

257] Pitch of a two start thread is 4 mm] Then the lead of the thread is given by -----

A] 4mm

B] 2mm

C] 8mm

D] 6mm

258] The Gear ratio required for cutting a screw thread of 2.5 mm on a lathe having a lead screw pitch using single point cutting tool is ----

A] 1:2

B] 2:1

C] 1:1 mm

259] The depth of cut for M24 x 3 mm internal thread is

A] 0.5412 x 3

B] 0.6134 x 3

C] 0.5 x 3

D] 0.7 x 3

260] To cut 24 x 3 mm internal acme threads, the core diameter of the job is

A] 20.00 mm

B] 21.66 mm

C] 21.00 mm

D] 20.60 mm

261] The depth of cut for metric square threading is

A] 0.6 x P

B] 0.5 x P

C] 0.5412 x P

D] 0.6412 x P

262] To cut buttress thread, the depth of cut is

A] 0.5412 x P

B] 0.6 x P

C] 0.7 x P

D] 0.75 x P

263] Which gauge is used to check the threading tool of lathe, for accuracy on the 60° angle?

A] Screw pitch gauge

B] Thread plug gauge

C] Centre gauge

D] Thread ring gauge

264] Slotting attachment converts .the rotary motion of spindle

A] vertical milling attachment is provided

B] can be turned through 90x in either direction

C] to increase the versatility' of the machine

265] Which one is the operation that cannot be done on the slotting machine?

A] key way slotting

B] dovetail slotting

C] gear cutting

D] <u>thread cutting</u>

266] Which one of the feed cannot be given to a slotter table with accessories

A] longitudinal

B] rotary

C] <u>vertical</u>

D] cross

267] The size of a slotter is specified by its maximum

A] longitudinal travel of table

B] height between table and ram

C] crosswise travel of table

D] length of stroke of ram

268] To slot a convex surface, the cutting tool required is

A] square nose tool

B] round nose tool

C] keyway tool

D] cornering tool

269] The convex surface can be slotted by using

A] longitudinal feed

B] rotary feed

C] cross feed

D] vertical feed

270] The purpose of quick return mechanism in a slotting machine is to

A] reduce the cutting time

B] have faster return stroke

C] maintain standard cutting speed

D] reduce idle time having faster idle stroke.

271] The main feed shaft of a slotting machine is drive by

A] bevel gear mechanism

B] pawl and ratchet wheel mechanism

C] tumbler gear mechanism.

D] worm and worm gear mechanism.

272] Loaded with spring

A] Plain or box type tool holder

B] Extension tool holder

C] Relieving type tool holder

D] Rotating tool holder]

273] For general purpose work

A] Plain or box type tool holder

B] Extension tool holder

C] Relieving type tool holder

D] Rotating tool holder]

274] Permits indexing for 90° at 4 positions

A] Plain or box type tool holder

B] Extension tool holder

C] Relieving type tool holder

D] Rotating tool holder]

275] For slotting larger circles

A] Plain or box type tool holder

B] Extension tool holder

C] Relieving type tool holder

D] Rotating tool holder]

276] Moves away the tool in the return stroke]

A] Plain or box type tool holder

B] Extension tool holder

C] Relieving type tool holder

D] Rotating tool holder]

277] Used on finished tubular surfaces to avoid marking

A] Stillson pipe wrench

B] Chain wrench

C] Strap wrench

D] Foot print wrench

278] Used for gripping and turning pipes and round stocks in confined pieces

A] Stillson pipe wrench

B] Chain wrench

C] Strap wrench

D] Foot print wrench

279] Used for holding large diameter pipes

A] Stillson pipe wrench

B] Chain wrench

C] Strap wrench

D] Foot print wrench

280] Used for gripping and turning pipes, tubes and cylindrical rods]

A] Stillson pipe wrench

B] Chain wrench

C] Strap wrench

D] Foot print wrench

281] The most important quality of any cutting fluid is

A] emulsification

B] specific heat

C] specific gravity

D] viscosity

282] By using coolants on workpieces we can choose

A] higher cutting speeds

B] lower cutting feeds

C] lower cutting speeds

D] heavy depth of cuts

283] Extreme pressure additive (EPA] is mixed with cutting fluid for improving its power of.

A] Cooling

B] Lubrication

D] Production of the machined surface

C] Cleaning of cutting zone

284] The main purpose for using a lubricant in machine tools is to ------

A] Cool down the making parts

B] Prevent machine tool from heating

C] Wet the making parts for close contact

D] Minimize the friction between the making parts

Types of Milling Machines

285] Spindle is perpendicular to the work table

A] Horizontal milling machine

B] Vertical milling machine

C] Universal milling machine]

D] Lathe machine

286] The table can be swivelled in horizontal plane

A] Horizontal milling machine

B] Vertical milling machine

C] Universal milling machine]

D] Lathe machine

287] The spindle is horizontal to the work table

A] Horizontal milling machine

B] Vertical milling machine

C] Universal milling machine]

D] Lathe machine

288] Rigid, sturdy and accommodates heavy work

A] Horizontal milling machine

B] Vertical milling machine

C] Universal milling machine]

D] Lathe machine

289] Boring, keyway cutting, profile milling can be done on this machine

A] Horizontal milling machine

B] Vertical milling machine

C] Universal milling machine]

D] Lathe machine

290] Helical grooves and gears can be milled on this machine.

A] Horizontal milling machine

B] Vertical milling machine

C] Universal milling machine]

D] Lathe machine

291] Slide movement on the column

A] Longitudinal feed

B] Cross feed

C] Vertical feed

D] Circular feed]

292] Slide movements on the knee

A] Longitudinal feed

B] Cross feed

C] Vertical feed

D] Circular feed]

293] Rotary table

A] Longitudinal feed

B] Cross feed

C] Vertical feed

D] Circular feed]

294] Table traverse]

A] Longitudinal feed

B] Cross feed

C] Vertical feed

D] Circular feed]

295] Long arbor threaded end is provided with left hand threads

A] To facilitate insertion of key between cutter and arbor at any position '

B] To facilitate positive power transmission to the arbor

C] To ' facilitate interchangeability of arbors and machines

D] To avoid loosening of arbor nut during cutting action]

296] Long arbor taper ends are as per ISO standards

A] To facilitate insertion of key between cutter and arbor at any position '

B] To facilitate positive power transmission to the arbor

C] To ' facilitate interchangeability of arbors and machines

D] To avoid loosening of arbor nut during cutting action]

297] Tennon slots are provided on arbor shoulder

A] To facilitate insertion of key between cutter and arbor at any position '

B] To facilitate positive power transmission to the arbor

C] To ' facilitate interchangeability of arbors and machines

D] To avoid loosening of arbor nut during cutting action]

298] Key slot is provided oh the entire arbor length]

A] To facilitate insertion of key between cutter and arbor at any position.

B] To facilitate positive power transmission to the arbor

C] To ' facilitate interchangeability of arbors and machines

D] To avoid loosening of arbor nut during cutting action]

299] produces surface perpendicular to the axis of cutter

A] is face milling process

B] is side milling process

C] is plain milling process

D] is end milling process

300] producing surfaces vertical and flat, perpendicular to the machine arbor

A] is face milling process

B] is side milling process

C] is plain milling process

D] is end milling process

301] cutting is done at end and periphery to make slots

A] is face milling process

B] is side milling process

C] is plain milling process

D] is end milling process

302] The process done on plain milling machine

A] is face milling process

B] is side milling process

C] is plain milling process

D] is end milling process

303] The process done on vertical milling machine.

A] is face milling process

B] is side milling process

C] is plain milling process

D] is end milling process

304] Composition of cobalt tungsten carbide and tentalum carbide

A] Carbon steel cutters

B] Sintered carbide tool cutters

C] Ceramics cutters

D] Diamond cutters

305] A composition of oxides of aluminium and silicon or magnesium

A] Carbon steel cutters

B] Sintered carbide tool cutters

C] Ceramics cutters

D] Diamond cutters

306] Steel with1.1%to 1.5% carbon

A] Carbon steel cutters

B] Sintered carbide tool cutters

C] Ceramics cutters

D] Diamond cutters

307] Suitable for low cutting speed and feed rates

A] Carbon steel cutters

B] Sintered carbide tool cutters

C] Ceramics cutters

D] Diamond cutters

308] Extremely high cutting speed with low feed rate for precision finishing]

A] Carbon steel cutters

B] Sintered carbide tool cutters

C] Ceramics cutters

D] Diamond cutters

309] More brittle in nature

A] Carbon steel cutters

B] Sintered carbide tool cutters

C] Ceramics cutters

D] Diamond cutters

310] is used to cut flutes on reamers

A] Equal double angle cutter

B] Bore type single angle cutter

C] Unequal double angle cutters

D] shank type single angle cutter]

311] is used to cut dovetail guide ways on a horizontal milling machine

A] Equal double angle cutter

B] Bore type single angle cutter

C] Unequal double angle cutters

D] shank type single angle cutter]

312] is used to cut 'V' grooves

A] Equal double angle cutter

B] Bore type single angle cutter

C] Unequal double angle cutters

D] shank type single angle cutter]

313] has two types as type 'A', type 'B' based on the diameter of the small end

A] Equal double angle cutter

B] Bore type single angle cutter

C] Unequal double angle cutters

D] shank type single angle cutter]

314] is Specified by mentioning two angles

A] Equal double angle cutter

B] Bore type single angle cutter

C] Unequal double angle cutters

D] shank type single angle cutter]

315] may or may not have cutting edges at flat side]

A] Equal double angle cutter

B] Bore type single angle cutter

C] Unequal double angle cutters

D] shank type single angle cutter]

316] Vertical milling attachment

A] face milling, boring, end drilling, ‘T’ slot milling

B] milling longer milling racks

C] mounted on the face of the column or the over arm

D] vertical milling attachment is provided

317] For using plain or universal milling machine as a vertical milling machine

A] face milling, boring, end drilling, ‘T’ slot milling

B] milling longer milling racks

C] mounted on the face of the column or the over arm

D] Vertical milling attachment is provided

318] Vertical attachments enable the horizontal milling machine to perform

A] face milling, boring, end drilling, ‘T’ slot milling

B] milling longer milling racks

C] mounted on the face of the column or the over arm

D] vertical milling attachment is provided

319] The rack milling attachment and rack indexing attachment used for

A] face milling, boring, end drilling, ‘T’ slot milling

B] milling longer milling racks

C] mounted on the face of the column or the over arm

D] vertical milling attachment is provided

320] Slotting attachment converts .the rotary motion of spindle

A] vertical milling attachment is provided

B] can be turned through 90x in either direction

C] to increase the versatility' of the machine

D] into reciprocating motion

321] Milling attachments are designed]

A] vertical milling attachment is provided

B] can be turned through 90x in either direction

C] to increase the versatility' of the machine

D] into reciprocating motion

322] attachment is useful involving light machining.

A] Gear cutting attachment

B] Spherical turning attachment

C] Relieving attachment]

D] None of above

323] tool advancement is] controlled by the cam profile.

A] Gear cutting attachment

B] Spherical turning attachment

C] Relieving attachment]

D] None of above

324] usefulforcutting splines etc.

A] Gear cutting attachment

B] Spherical turning attachment

C] Relieving attachment]

D] None of above

326] The jig bush used for drilling and reaming of a hole is...?

A] Press fit bush

B] Liner bush

C] Slip renewable bush

D] Fixed renewable bush

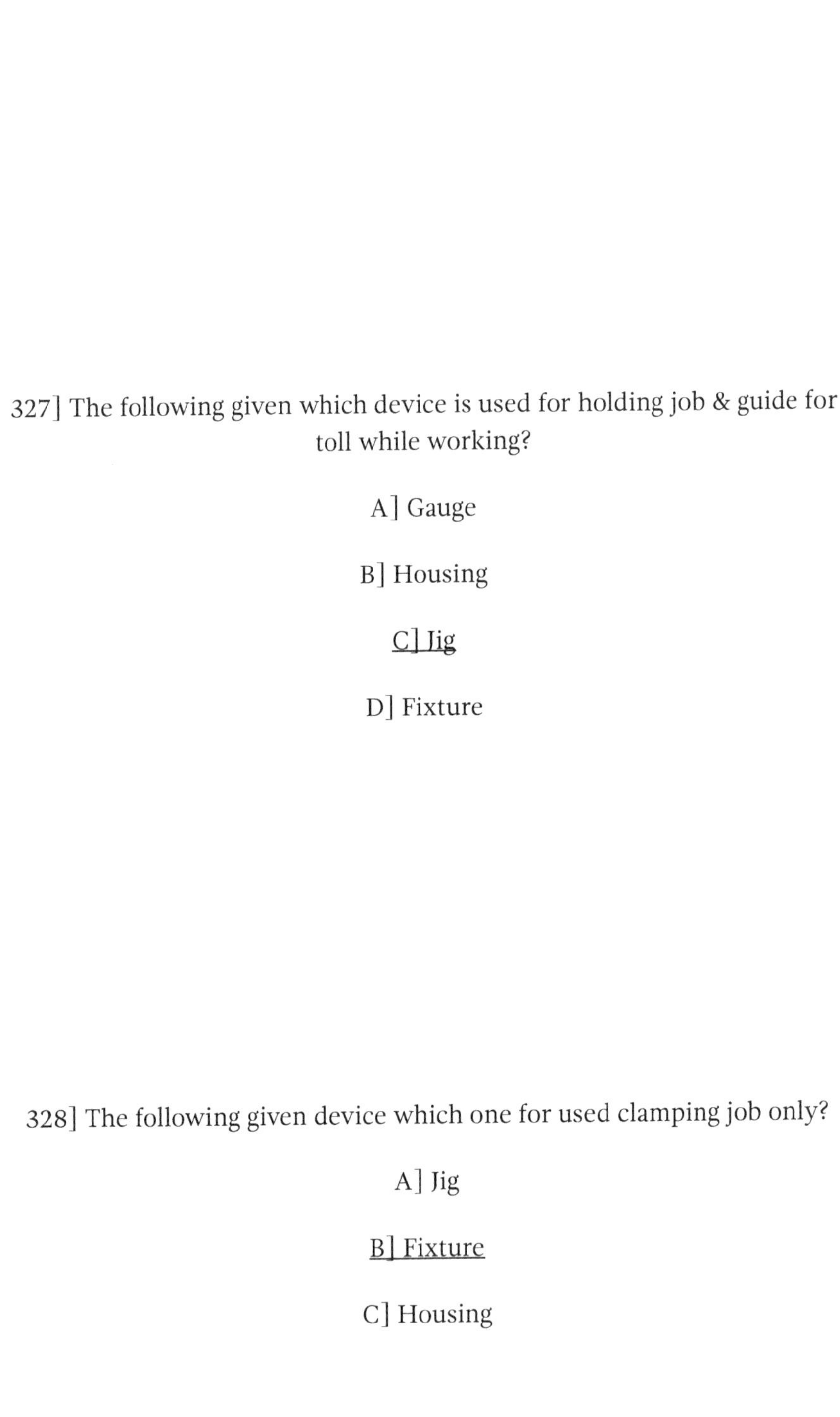

327] The following given which device is used for holding job & guide for toll while working?

A] Gauge

B] Housing

C] Jig

D] Fixture

328] The following given device which one for used clamping job only?

A] Jig

B] Fixture

C] Housing

D] Gauge

329] While fabricated by welding job which device is used for holding fixed or revolving if necessary up to 360°C of welding job?

A] Gauge

b] Template

C] Jig

<u>D] Fixture</u>

330] The main things of drilling jig its not clamping with machine table which reason is correct given following?

<u>A] it is strong for operation</u>

B] it is easy for operation

C] many different size holes produce by different setting while drilling on job

D] for this device has lot of time

331] Following which locations is most usefull for round shape job location?

A] pin type locator

B] wedge type locator

<u>C] vee locator</u>

D] adjustable stop locators

332] Following which reason is correct for using bushing in drilling jigs?

A] easy for drilling

B] for fixed drill hole size

C] for accurate drilling operation

D] for given better finish drilling hole

333] The metal for manufacturing jig bush is...?

A] mild steel

B] cast iron

C] cast steel

D] tool steel

334] Given following bush which busing used for locating renewable bushing?

A] press fit bushing

B] linear bushing

C] special bushing

D] knurd bushing

335] jig has tolerance..?

A] five present of job tolerance

B] ten percent of job tolerance

C] 20% to 50% of job tolerance

D] 100% of job tolerance

336] Following which jig is use for location from bore?

A] plate jig

B] solid jig

C] post jig

D] box jig

337] Following which jig having drill plate?

A] solid jig

B] plate jig

C] box jig

D] table jig

338] Following which locator is used for internal diameter location?

A] solid saports

B] Pin type locator

C] Vee locator

D] nest locator

339] Drm jig bushing-are generally hardened to ------------]

A] Mild steel

B] Cast iron

C] Cast steel

D] Tooi steel

340] Jigs is device which -------------

A] Locate the work piece

B] Holding and supporting the work piece

C] Guide the cutting tool

D] Does all the above

341] Which among the following jigs is used forllocation from a bore?

A] Plate jig

B] Solid jig

C] Post jig

D] Box jig

342] Fixture is a production device which -----------]

A] Holds and locate the work piece

B] Holds the piece

C] Chats the work piece,

D] Neither holds nor] Locates the-work piece

343] Which one of the following is used to guide tool and hold the job in mass production? '

A] Gauge]

B] Housing

C] Fixture

D] Jig

344] Which among the following is the purpose for proi/iding bushing in a drill jig?

A] For locating accurately and guiding the drill for precise drilling operation

B] For determining the size of the hole to be drilled

C] For easy drilling

D] For getting good finished surface in the drilled holes

345] Drill jig are used for? _

A] Drill operations only]

B] Clamping the job for drilling

C] Drilling, Reaming, Tapping and other operations

D] Guiding the tools only

346] Which one of the following jigs consists of drill plate, which rests on the component to be drilled?

A] Solid jig]

B] Plate jig]

C] Box jig

D] Trunnion jig

347] Jig is a device which -----------

A] Locates the work piece]

B] Hold and supports the work piece and guides tool

C] Guides the cutting tool

D] Hold the cutting tool]

348] Drill jig are used for

A] Drilling, reaming, tapping and other allied operations

B] Drilling operations only

C] Clamping the job when drilling

D] Guiding the tool only

349] Fixture is a production device which---------: -----

A] holds the work piece ‘

B] Locate the work piece

C] Holds and locates the work piece

D] Neither holds nor locates the work piece

350] Purpose of the Box Jig is to

A] Hold the job and guide the tool to produce internal threads

B] To produce many inclined holes

C] To produce many straight holes

D] None of these

351] Jigs and fixtures are --------]

A] Machining tools

B] Precision tools

C] Both (a] & (b]

D] None of these

352] 'How jig are in terms of weight compared to fixtures?

A] Jigs are lighter than fixtures

B] Jigs are heavier than fixtures

C] jigs are equal in weight to fixtures for same operation

D] None of these

353] Which fixtures are used for machining parts which musthav-e machined details evenw spaced?

A] Profile fixtures

B] Duplex fixtures

C] Indexing fixtures

D] None of these

354] Main purpose Of annealing is -----------]

A] to improve machinability

B] to improve magnetism

C] to increase hardness

D] to increase toughness

355] The carbon percentage in H.S.S] tool is -------

A] 0.75 to 1.00 %

B] 1.00 to 2.00 00

C] 0.60 to 0.75 %

D] 0.02 to 0.03 %]

356] Which one of the following is the resistance of a metal to elastic deformation?

A] Ductility]

B] Strength

C] Stiffness

D] Toughness

357] The process of heating and cooling to change the structure of steel for obtaining the required properties is called

A] Hardening

B] Normalizing

C] Heat treatment

D] Tempering

358] The main purpose of annealing is to

A] Increase the hardness

B] Increase the toughness

C] Improve machinability

D] Improve distortion

359] The purpose of normalizing steel is to -----------

A] Remove the induced Stress

B] Improve genes and reduce brittleness

C] Soften the metal

D] Increase the surface?

360] Which one of the following process is used for hardenmg the outer 5” Annealing

A] Hardening

B] Tempering

C] Case Hardening

D] Tear surface

361] The purpose of producmg a component with tough and ductIle core and hard ou is known as.]

A] Hardening

B] Case hardening

C] Tempering

D] annealing

362] Lower critical temperature of high carbon steel while hardening is ----------

A] 9600C

B] 900°C

c] 7230 c

D] 56O C

363] The process of Changing the structure and thus changing the properties by heating and ‘cooling is known as --

A] Heat treatment

B] Alloying

C] Tempering

D] None of these

364] For refining the grain structure which one of the following heat treatment processes 'Is adopted]

A] Annealing

B] Hardening

C] Tempering

D] Normalising

365] Annealing is performed on iron and steel ---------

A] To remove internal stresses

B] To reduce hardness

C] To improve machinability

D] All of these

366] Which one of the following does not fall under the stages of heat treatment?

A] Heating

B] Cleaning

C] Quenching

D] Soaking

20] METAL 02

367] Gun metal is an alloy of copper, ------------

A] tin and zinc

B] Lead and zinc

C] Zinc and nickel

D] Lead and nickel

368] for making gutters, roof flashing, hoods etc]

A] Galvanised iron

B] Stainless steel

C] Copper sheet

D] Metal sheets

369] in dairies] food processing, kitchen ware etc]

A] Galvanised iron

B] Stainless steel

C] Copper sheet

D] Metal sheets

370] for making buckets, heating ducts, cabinets etc]

A] Galvanised iron

B] Stainless steel

C] Copper sheet

D] Metal sheets

371] in canneries and chemical plants Metal sheets

A] Galvanised iron

B] Stainless steel

C] Copper sheet

D] Metal sheets

372] Alloy steel, good corrosive resistance and welds easily

A] Black iron

B] Galvanised iron

C] Stainless steel

D] Aluminium

373] Cheapest, can be rolled to any desired thickness

A] Black iron

B] Galvanised iron

C] Stainless steel

D] Aluminium

374] Resists against rust bright silvery appearance

A] Black iron

B] Galvanised iron

C] Stainless steel

D] Aluminium

375] Corrodes rapidly] Bluish black appearance

A] Black iron

B] Galvanised iron

C] Stainless steel

D] Aluminium

376] Hardness of grinding wheel is determine by ----------

A] the resistance exerted] by the bond against grinding Stress

B] Hardness of abrasive grains

C] Hardness of bond

D] Ability to penetration

377] When it is required to run a Grinding wheel safely at very high speed, which bond should be used? "

A] Vitrified

B] Shellac

C] Silicate

D] resinoid' and rubber

378] in surface grinding what is the suitable range of grain size of the grinding wheel for general purpose surface grinding?

A] 20 to 36

B] 46 to 60

C] 80 to 120

D] 150 to 300

379] AS per Indian Standard, the grain '46'.comes under the group of «w] -----

A] Coarse

B] Medium

C] Fine

D] Very fine

380] The grit size of the abrasives used in the grinding wheel is usually specified by ----------

A] Hardness number

B] A size of wheel

C] Softness or hardness of the abrasive

D] Mesh number

381] Bench grinder are used for

A] Heavy duty work

B] Heavy and light duty work

C] Light duty work

D] Lather work

382] Bench Grinders are fitted on a

A] Base

B] Table]

C] Wheel guards

D] Conveyor

383] Which one of the following is the most commonly used Precision grinding machines?

A] Surface grinders

B] Tool cutter grinders

C] Cylindrical grinders

D] All of these

384] Surface grinding machine table slides over the ----------

A] 'T' __ 5.0.:

B] 'v' slot

C] 'U' slot

D] Radial slot

385] Thc purposc of the surface grinder is to

A] Produce curved surface

B] Produce flat surfaces

C] Produce cylindrical surface

D] Produce uneven surface

386] The cylindrical grinding produced may be

A] plain, cylinder and stepped

B] Plan, tapered and cylinder

C] Cylinder, tapered and stepped

387] Used for rapid method of indexing.

A] Direct indexing head

B] Simple indexing head

C] Universal indexing head

D] None of above

388] Used where a large number of identical pieces are indexed

A] Direct indexing head

B] Simple indexing head

C] Universal indexing head

D] None of above

389] Used with a number of change of gears for differential indexing]

A] Direct indexing head

B] Simple indexing head

C] Universal indexing head

D] None of above

390] Grinding wheels made out of---------------- abrasive are most common because of its free and cool cutting action]

A] Aluminium oxide

B] Silicon oxide

C] Ammonium oxide

D] Carbide]

391] Which among the following abrasive is mostly used for cutting off wheels for cutting non metallic materials?

A] Aluminium oxide

B] Silicon carbide

C] Diamond

D] None of above

392] Which abrasive particle is used for grinding tungsten carbide tool insert?

A] Silicon carbide

B] A|203

C] Diamond

D] Corundum

393] Which of the following is the natural abrasive?

A] Aluminium oxide

B] Silicon

C] Boron carbide

D] Corundum

394] Which of the following is the manufactured abrasive?

A] Corundum]

B] Quartz

C] Silicon

D] Emery

395] Which abrasive particle is used for grinding steel fittings?

A] Silicon carbide

B] Aluminium oxide

C] Diamond]

D] boron oxide

396] What kind of abrasive cut of wheel should be used to cut concrete stone and masonry?

A] Silicon

B] Al203

C] Diamond grit

D] Glass

397] Aluminium oxide wheel is used for grinding -----------

A] cast iron

B] Cemented carbide.

C] HSS '

D] ceramic

398] The bond of diamond wheel suitable for offhand grinding of the tipped tool is

A] Resinoid

B] Vitrified

C] Shellac

D] Metal

399] Which among the following bonds, is used commonly?

A] Vitrified bond '

B] Rubber bond

C] Shellac bond

D] Silicate bond

400] The symbol conventionally used for resinoid .bond is ~~~~~~~~

A] v

B] R f

C] B

D] E

401] In grinding practice the term "grade of wheel" refers to ---------'

A] Hardness of the abrasive used

B] Strength of the bond of the wheel

C] Finish 0f the Wheel

D] Hardness of the work pieces

402] Which bond is used in cut of wheels?

A] Rubber

B] Vitrified

C] Resirjoid

D] Shellac

INDUSTRIAL TRAINING INSTITUTE

Monthly Test-1, Marks- 20, Date:- _______________

(Every Question Carry Two Marks)

1-06] in case of an accident, the victim should im

A] Asked to take rest

C] Attended immediately

D] leave him

2-07] First aid is given to an injured or ill person primarily

A] Save life

B] Prevent further deterioration of the muff's

C] Give best possible comfort

D] All of these

3-08] Colour code for Bins for waste paper segregation is -----

A] blue Colour

B] Yellow Colour

C] Red Colour

D] Green Colour

4-09] Which one is a workshop safety?

A] Keep shop floor clean and free from grease, oil or other slippery materials

B] Stop the machine before changing the speed

C] Don't use cracked or chipped tools

D] Don't try to stop a running machine with hand

5-10] In Personal Protect Equipment (PPE] HELMET is used to

A] protect head

B] Protect eyes

C] Protect hands

D] Protect ears

6-11] Which of the following belongs to general safety?

A Have a worker in good attitude

B] The work clean and clear

C] Concentrate on your work

D] Keep the floor and gangways clean and clear

7-12] While grinding, which is used to protect the eyes?

A] Dark green glass

B] Mask

C] Sun glasses

D] Safety goggles

8-13] Which of the following is done for machine safety?

A] Check the oil level before starting the machine

B] Do things in a methodical way

C] Keep the floor and gangways clean and clear

D] Don't use dies and scarves

9-14] ln Personal Protect Equipment (PPE., 'sleeves' is used to protect ----------

A] Face

B] Eyes

C] Ears

D] Hands

10-15] ABC stands for --------------

A] Automatic Breathing Control

B] Automatic Blood Control

C] Airway Breathing Circulation

D] Automatic Blood Circulation

INDUSTRIAL TRAINING INSTITUTE

Monthly Test-2, Marks- 20, Date:- _______________

(Every Question Carry Two Marks)

1-21] The instrument used to mark parallel lines, parallel to the datum edge is -

A] jenny caliper

B] Divider

C] Outside calliper

D] Inside calliper

2-22] Which one of the following is an indirect measuring tool?

A] Outside caliper

B] Vernier calliper

C] Steel rule

D] Outside micrometer

3 23] For cutting thin tubing, the most suitable pitch of the hacksaw blade is...

A] 1.8mm

B] 1.4mm

C] 1mm

D] 0.8mm

4-24] For cutting solid brass, the most suitable pitch of the hacksaw blade is...

A] 1.8mm

B] 1.4mm

C] 1mm

D] 0.8mm

5-25] A new hacksaw blade after a few strokes becomes loose because of the...

A] Stretching of the blade

B] Wing-nut threads being worn out

C] Wrong pitch of the blade

D] Improper selection of the set of saws.

6-26] While cutting small diameter pipes, it is advisable to watch regularly and ensure that...

A] The cut is along the curved line

B] More saw teeth are in contract

C] The work is not overheated

D] Proper balancing of hacksaw is maintained

7-27] The vice clamps are used to

A] Protect hard jaws

B] Clamp the work pieces rigidly

C] Protect the finished surfaces

D] Prevent the movable jaw being filed

8-28] The reference surface during marking is provided by the...

A] Surface gauge

B] Workpiece

C] Drawing of the work

D] Marking table surface

9-29] The size of an engineer's vice is specified by the

A] Length of the movable jaw

B] Width of the jaws

C] Height of the vice

D] Maximum opening of the jaws

10-30] The part of the universal surface gauge which helps to draw a parallel line along a datum edge is the...

A] Rocker arm

B] Snug

C] Fine adjustment screw

D] Guide pins

INDUSTRIAL TRAINING INSTITUTE

Monthly Test-3, Marks- 20, Date:- _______________

(Every Question Carry Two Marks)

1-36] 'V' blocks are available in grades of...

A] A & B

B] A,B & C

C] 1,2 & 3

D] 1 & 2

2-37] 'V' blocks of grade 'B' are made of

A] Cast iron

B] Mild steel

C] Steel

D] Cast steel

3-38] Name the punch used to locate the centre

A] Prick punch 30°

B] Prick punch 60°

C] Centre punch

D] Dot punch

4-39] The point angle of centre punch is --------

A] 30°

B] 50°

c] 900

D] 1200

5-40] Punches are used for forming ---------of any shape

A] Holes

B] Mining

C] Knurling

D] Reaming

6-41] Generally the length of the handle of the vice is ----------

A] 1.5 times the normal size of the vice

B] 2.5 times the normal size of the vice

C] 3.5 times the normal size of the vice

D] 4.5 times the normal size of the vice

7-42] Bench vice spindle is made of

A] mild steel

B] Cast iron

C] Tool steel

D] Bronze

8-43] The convexity of files helps

A] To file concave surfaces

B] To file convex surfaces

C] To prevent rounding of edges of work

D] The file to become straight when pressure is applied

9-44] Which file used for filling wood, leather and other soft material?]

A] Single cut file

B] Double cut file

c] Rasp cut file

D] Curved cut file

10-45] File used is used for ------------

A] Cleaning the work piece

C] Renewing the file teeth

B] cleaning the file teeth

D] Cleaning the chips

INDUSTRIAL TRAINING INSTITUTE

Monthly Test-4, Marks- 20, Date:- _______________

(Every Question Carry Two Marks)

1-51] Aluminium oxide wheel is used for grinding ------------

A] cast iron

B] Cemented carbide.

C] HSS '

D] ceramic

2-52] The bond of diamond wheel suitable for offhand grinding of the tipped tool is

A] Resinoid

B] Vitrified

C] Shellac

D] Metal

3-53] Which among the following bonds, is used commonly?

A] Vitrified bond '

B] Rubber bond

C] Shellac bond

D] Silicate bond

4-54] The symbol conventionally used for resinoid .bond is ~~~~~~~~

A] v

B] R f

C] B

D] E

5-55] In grinding practice the term "grade of wheel" refers to ---------'

A] Hardness of the abrasive used

B] Strength of the bond of the wheel

C] Finish 0f the Wheel

D] Hardness of the work pieces

6-56] Which bond is used in cut of wheels?

A] Rubber

B] Vitrified

C] Resirjoid

D] Shellac

7-57] Grinding wheels made out of---------------- abrasive are most common because of its free and cool cutting action]

A] Aluminium oxide

B] Silicon oxide

C] Ammonium oxide

D] Carbide]

8-58] Which among the following abrasive is mostly used for cutting off wheels for cutting non metallic materials?

A] Aluminium oxide

B] Silicon carbide

C] Diamond

D] None of above

9-59] Which abrasive particle is used for grinding tungsten carbide tool insert?

A] Silicon carbide

B] A|203

C] Diamond

D] Corundum

10-60] Which of the following is the natural abrasive?

A] Aluminium oxide

B] Silicon

C] Boron carbide

D] Corundum

INDUSTRIAL TRAINING INSTITUTE

Monthly Test-5, Marks- 20, Date:- ______________

(Every Question Carry Two Marks)

1-66] in surface grinding what is the suitable range of grain size of the grinding wheel for general purpose surface grinding?

A] 20 to 36

B] 46 to 60

C] 80 to 120

D] 150 to 300

2-67] AS per Indian Standard, the grain '46'.comes under the group of «w] -----

A] Coarse

B] Medium

C] Fine

D] Very fine

3-68] The grit size of the abrasives used in the grinding wheel is usually specified by ----------

A] Hardness number

B] A size of wheel

C] Softness or hardness of the abrasive

D] Mesh number

4-69] Bench grinder are used for

A] Heavy duty work

B] Heavy and light duty work

C] Light duty work

D] Lather work

5-70] Bench Grinders are fitted on a

A] Base

B] Table]

C] Wheel guards

D] Conveyor

6-71] The taper shank drills are held on the machine by means of...

A] Chucks

B] Sleeves

C] Drift

D] Vice

7-72] Drill chucks are fitted on the drilling machine spindle by means of a...

A] Knurled ring

B] Arbor

C] Drift

D] Pinion and key

8-73] The Morse taper provided on drills ranges between

A] MT 1 to MT 5

B] MT 1 to MT 4

C] MT 0 to MT 5

D] MT 0 to MT 4

9-74] A drift is used for...

A] Drawing a drill location

B] Fixing chuck on the machine spindle

C] Removing a broken drill from the work

D] Removing the drill from the machine spindle

10-75] When the taper shank of the drill is larger than the machine spindle, the device to hold the drill is a...

A] Drill sleeve

B] Taper socket

C] Drill drift

D] Chuck and key

INDUSTRIAL TRAINING INSTITUTE

Monthly Test-6, Marks- 20, Date:- ______________

(Every Question Carry Two Marks)

1-81] The clearance angle of the drill is between

A] 3? to 5?

B] 8? to 12?

C] 12? to 20?

D] 15? to 20?

2-82] In a remote place (no electricity available] a rail track is to be drilled] Choose the right drilling machine

A] Radial drilling machine

B] Pillar drilling machine

C] Ratchet drilling machine

D] Sensitive drilling Machine

3-83] A drilling machine used by a carpenter for cabinet making is a

A] Ratchet drilling machine

B] Radial drilling machine

C] Breast drilling machine

D] Sensitive drilling machine

4-84] Which one of the following drilling machines is used for drilling holes where electricity is not available?

A] Bench drilling machine

B] Pillar drilling machine

C] Redial drilling machine

D] Ratchet drilling machine

5-85] Which one of the following drilling machine is used for heavy duty work?

A] Bench drilling machine

B] Pillar drilling machine

C] Radial drilling machine

D] Electric hand drilling machine

6-86] Drill chuck are held on the machine spindle by means of ------

A] arbor

B] Drift

C] draw-in bar

D] Chuck nut

7-87] Different speeds are obtained in a sensitive bench drilling machine by ----

A] Belt pulley mechanism

B] Hydraulic mechanism

C] Rack and Pinion mechanism

D] Cam and follower mechanism

8-88] The tapping drill size for M10 x 15 is ----------

A] 8.2

B] 8.3

C] 8.4

D] 8.5

9-89] A nut is to be made for a screw of M10XI.S] What should be the size of drilled hole?

A] 8-5 mm

B] 9.0 mm

C] 9.5 mm

D] 10.0 mm

10-90] Tap are re-sharpened by grinding

A] Flutes

B] Threads

C] Diameter

D] Relief

INDUSTRIAL TRAINING INSTITUTE

Monthly Test-7, Marks- 20, Date:- _______________

(Every Question Carry Two Marks)

1-96] A die in which cutting and non cutting operations are carried out per stroke.

A] Piercing die

B] Progressive die

C] Combination die

D] Compound die

2-97] A die in which two or more sequential operations are performed at two or more stations upon the work.

A] Piercing die

B] Progressive die

C] Combination die

D] Compound die

3-98] A die in which the shape of the punch and die are directly reproduced in the metal with little or no metal flow.

A] Progressive die

B] Combination die

C] Compound die

D] Forming die

4-99] The die used for producing any shape of holes.

A] Piercing die

B] Progressive die

C] Combination die

D] Compound die

5-100] A short reamer with an axial hole used with an arbor or mandrel is called -------

A] Parallel reamer

B] Adjustable reamer

C] Expansion reamer

D] Chucking reamer

6-101] Which one of the following machine reamers is used to correct the misalignment between the reamer axis and the work axis?

A] Floating blade reamer

B] Machine jig reamer]

C] Shell reamer

D] Chucking reamer

7-102] The least count of a vernier height gauge in the metric system is

A] 0.05 mm

B] 0.1 mm

C] 0.02 mm

D] 0.001 mm

8-103] The least count of a vernier height gauge in the british system is

A] 0.05”

B] 0.001"

C] 0.002"

D] 1"

9-104] For marking purposes, a vernier height gauge must be used on the

A] bed of a machine tool

B] surface plate

C] square block

D] any flat surface

10105] The reading of a vernier height gauge is similar to that of a

A] vernier caliper

B] depth micrometer

C] dial test indicator

D] gauge

INDUSTRIAL TRAINING INSTITUTE

Monthly Test-8, Marks- 20, Date:- ______________

(Every Question Carry Two Marks)

1-111] The maximum clearance required between hole'30 +0..021, 0.000 and shaft 30 -0.110, 0.143 is.

A] 0.110 mm '

B.0.131 mm

C] 0.164 mm

D] 0.143 mm

2-112] A dimension is stated as 25 .1002 mm in a drawing] What is the tolerance?

A] +0.02 mm'

B] +0.04 mm

C] -0.02 mm

D] 25.00 mm

3-113] A pin is fitted in a hole] The tolerance zone of the pin is entirely above that of hole] The fit obtained will be?

A] Clearance fit

B] Transition fit

C] Interference fit

D] Running fit

4-114] Tolerance is given to the part size to

A] Production the part within the required permissible size error

B] Increase the production

C] Decrease the Production

D] Finish the components approximately

5-115] Which one of the following is the clearance fit under the whole basic system?

A] 20 H7/p6'

B] 2067/211

C] ZOG/gll

D] 20H/g11

6-116] The three classes of fits as per BIS system aré

A] Clearance fit, interference fit and transition fit

B] Medium fit, push fit and tight fit

C] Flat fit, round fit and square fit

D] 'Sliding fit ', loose fit and shrinkage fit

7-117] Which one of the following tolerance specifications has a maximum dimensionless than 20 mm?

A] 20 +0.2,-0.3

B] 20 320.2

C] 20 -0.2, 0.3 e

D.m 20 +500, ~03

8 118] Difference between the maximum and minimum limit is ------------------

A] Single informant

B] Basic shaft

C] Clearance

D] Tolerance

9-119] A shaft 55 running freely in bush bearing the type of fit is ---------

A] Clearance fit

B] Driving plate

C] shrinkage fit

D] None of the above

10-120] The least count of vernier calliper is (main scale = 49 division, vernier scale = 50 division]

A] 0.1 mm

B] 0.01 mm

C] 0.001 mm

D] 0.02 mm

INDUSTRIAL TRAINING INSTITUTE

Monthly Test-9, Marks- 20, Date:- ______________

(Every Question Carry Two Marks)

1-126] The value of the smallest division on sleeve of a metric outside micrometer is -----

A] 0.50 mm

B] 1.00 mm

C] 1.50 mm

D] 2.00 mm

2-127] Ratchet stop in the micrometer helps to --------

A] control the pressure

B] Lock the spindle

C] Adjust the zero error

D] Hold the work piece

3-128} Uses of a dial test indicator are ----------

A] To check plane surface for parallelism and flatness

B] To check the straightness of shaft and bars

C] To check concentricity of holes and shafts

D] All the above

4-129] The dial test indicators shows that the measurement as -------

A] The magnified small variation is size through a point

B] The difference between the top steps of the 5 mm

C] The actual size of the component

D] The direct reading of the dimension

5-130] Name the instrument which magnifies the small variation is size measured]

A] Vernier calliper

B] Micrometer

C] Dial indicator

D] Steel rule

6-131] The cutting speed for aluminium with H.S.S] tools is

A.] 30 m/min

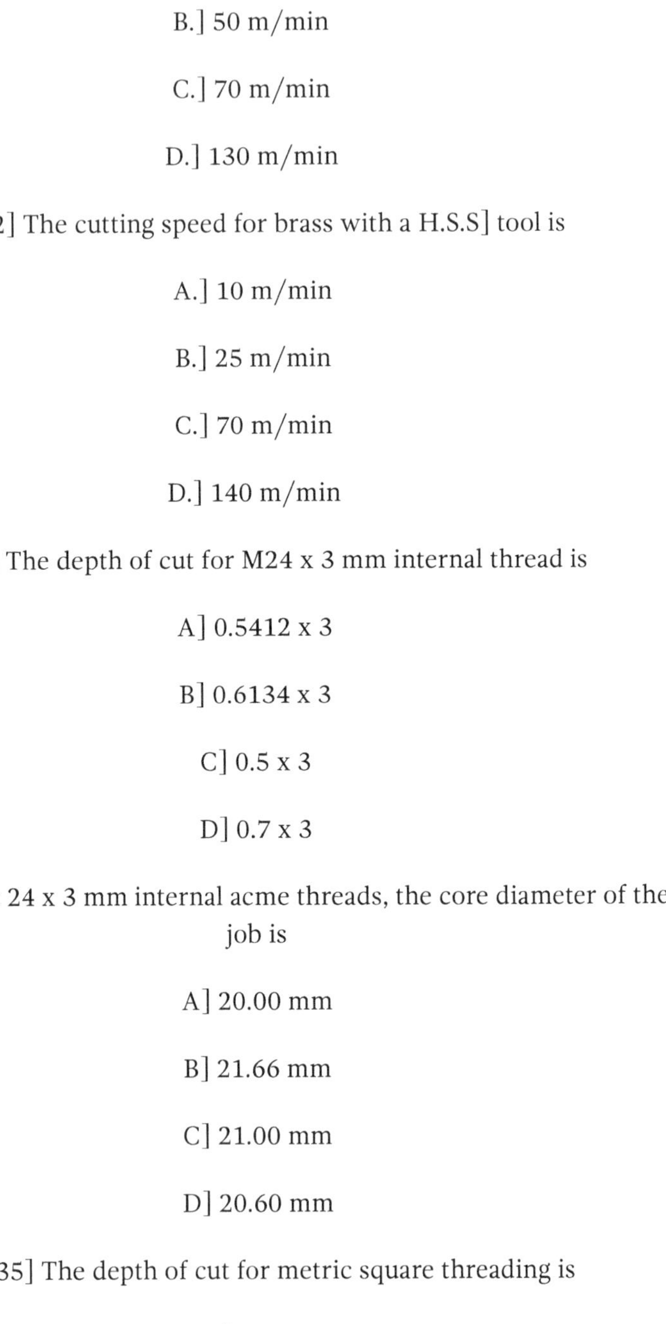

B.] 50 m/min

C.] 70 m/min

D.] 130 m/min

7-132] The cutting speed for brass with a H.S.S] tool is

A.] 10 m/min

B.] 25 m/min

C.] 70 m/min

D.] 140 m/min

8-133] The depth of cut for M24 x 3 mm internal thread is

A] 0.5412 x 3

B] 0.6134 x 3

C] 0.5 x 3

D] 0.7 x 3

9-134] To cut 24 x 3 mm internal acme threads, the core diameter of the job is

A] 20.00 mm

B] 21.66 mm

C] 21.00 mm

D] 20.60 mm

10-135] The depth of cut for metric square threading is

A] 0.6 x P

B] 0.5 x P

C] 0.5412 x P

D] 0.6412 x P

INDUSTRIAL TRAINING INSTITUTE

Monthly Test-10, Marks- 20, Date:- ______________

(Every Question Carry Two Marks)

1-141] For mass-production which machine is used?

A] Centre Lathe

B] Production Lathe

C] Special Lathe

D] Engine Lathe

2-142] Which lathe is used for more accurate job?

A] Centre Lathe

B] Special Lathe

C] Production Lathe

D] Tool Room Lathe

3-143] The accuracy of Tool Room Lathe is to Compeer Centre Lathe.]

(A] Less

(B] More

(C] Very Less

(D] Equal

4-144] In Locomotive Assemble Wheel with Axel is turning on Lathe

(A] Centre Lathe

(B] Tool Room Lathe

(C] Wheel Lathe

(D] Gap Bed Lathe

5-145] Cast iron is used for manufacturing machine beds because -------

A] it can resist more compressive stress

B] it is heavy in weight

C] It is cheaper metal

D] It is a brittle metal

6-146] Which one of the following operations can't be performed on a Center Lathe?]

A] Turning

B] Thread cutting

C] Gear cutting

D] Taper turning

7-147] The cutting edge of a solid tool is made of

A] carbon steel

B] mild steel

C] super high speed steel

D] stelite

8-148] The tip of a cemented carbide threading tool is

A] brazed

B] welded

C] soldered

D] clamped to the shank

9-149] Tool will rub against the work surfaces and the cutting force increases when..

A] The clearance angle is more

B] The clearance angel is less

C] The rake angle is more

D] The rake angle is less

10-150] Formation of a chip while cutting is based on the...

A] Rake angle of the tool

B] Clearance angle of the tool

C] Wedge angle of the tool

D] Clearance and wedge angle of the tool

INDUSTRIAL TRAINING INSTITUTE

Monthly Test-11, Marks- 20, Date:- _______________

(Every Question Carry Two Marks)

1-156] What happen if cutting tool setting done lower of center height?

A] Encrease top Rake angle

B] Decrease top Rake angle

C] No any effect on to Rake

D] Decrease clearance angle

2-157] If cutting tool is upsetting of centre of job?

A] Encrease front clearance angle

B] Decrease front clearance angle

C] no any effect on front clearance angle

D] none of them

3-158] If cutting tool is down setting of centre of job?

A] Front clearance angle is increase

B] Front clearance angle is decrease

C] No any effect on clearance angle

D] None of them

4-159] Zero Rake angle give for tool?

A] To avoid friction of tool

B] For increase tool life

C] For increase straight of tool

D] For better finishing on job

5-160] For carbide tip tool turning on hard material it has......essential?

A] Side Rake angle

B] Zero Rake angle

C] Positive Rake angle

D] Negative Rake angle

6-161] For do not break cutting edge of cutting tool...?

A] Feed increase

B] Cutting speed done low

C] Length of nose decrease

D] Use negative rake angle

7-162] Chip breaker in a tool is given

A] 'It break the chips into small pieces

B] to have continuous type of chips from long cut

C] to have crushed chips]

8-163] Step type chip breaker is the one

A] in which a small groove is ground behind the cutting edge

B] in which a step IS ground on the face of the tool along the cutting edge

C] in which a thin carbide plate or clamp is brazed or screwed on the face of the tool]

9-164] For mounting a lathe chuck

A] start it by hand and then turn the power on

B] mount it on by power

C] mount it by hand

D] mount it with the help of a hammer

10-165] The least count of a vernier bevel protractor is...

A] 1"

B] 5'

C] 1?

D] 5 ?

INDUSTRIAL TRAINING INSTITUTE

Monthly Test-12, Marks- 20, Date:- ______________

(Every Question Carry Two Marks)

1-388] Used where a large number of identical pieces are indexed

A] Direct indexing head

B] Simple indexing head

C] Universal indexing head

D] None of above

2-389] Used with a number of change of gears for differential indexing]

A] Direct indexing head

B] Simple indexing head

C] Universal indexing head

D] None of above

3-390] Grinding wheels made out of---------------- abrasive are most common because of its free and cool cutting action]

A] Aluminium oxide

B] Silicon oxide

C] Ammonium oxide

D] Carbide]

4-391] Which among the following abrasive is mostly used for cutting off wheels for cutting non metallic materials?

A] Aluminium oxide

B] Silicon carbide

C] Diamond

D] None of above

5-392] Which abrasive particle is used for grinding tungsten carbide tool insert?

A] Silicon carbide

B] A|203

C] Diamond

D] Corundum

6-393] Which of the following is the natural abrasive?

A] Aluminium oxide

B] Silicon

C] Boron carbide

D] Corundum

7-394] Which of the following is the manufactured abrasive?

A] Corundum]

B] Quartz

C] Silicon

D] Emery

8-395] Which abrasive particle is used for grinding steel fittings?

A] Silicon carbide

B] Aluminium oxide

C] Diamond]

D] boron oxide

9-396] What kind of abrasive cut of wheel should be used to cut concrete stone and masonry?

A] Silicon

B] Al203

C] Diamond grit

D] Glass

10-397] Aluminium oxide wheel is used for grinding ------------

A] cast iron

B] Cemented carbide.

C] HSS '

D] ceramic

www.ingramcontent.com/pod-product-compliance
Ingram Content Group UK Ltd.
Pitfield, Milton Keynes, MK11 3LW, UK
UKHW021909190726
13853UKWH00002B/588

9 798888 696873